Evidence based practices made easy

An easy, practical emotional regulation guide with a combination of DBT, Shadow Work and IFS

Acknowledgements

To everyone who has ever felt "too emotional," "too reactive," or "too much";
this workbook was built with you in mind.

Thank you to the people who have trusted me with their questions, their stories, and their moments of honesty. Your courage and curiosity shaped every page.

Thank you to the clinicians and researchers who paved the way for DBT, IFS, and lived experience inclusion. Their work helped many of us understand ourselves with far more clarity and compassion.

And thank you to my younger self who kept searching for answers long before she had the words for what she needed.

This book exists because so many of us were never taught how to feel safe in our own minds and bodies.

I'm grateful you're here, taking this step for yourself.

You are not a monster.
Your traits are manageable.
You are not alone.

Disclaimer and permissions

Disclaimer

This workbook is designed to support emotional regulation and self-understanding. It is not a substitute for professional mental health care, diagnosis, or crisis support. Move through each section gently and pause whenever you need. Use these exercises alongside your existing support system.

If You Need Immediate Support

Australia: Lifeline 13 11 14 • Beyond Blue 1300 224 636 • 000 in an emergency

United States: 988 Suicide & Crisis Lifeline • Crisis Text HOME to 741741

United Kingdom: Samaritans 116 123 • NHS mental health helplines

If your region is not listed, search for "mental health crisis line" in your country.

Dialectical Behavior Therapy (DBT) Notice

DBT was created by Dr. Marsha Linehan. This workbook is inspired by DBT principles but is not an official DBT program and is not affiliated, supervised, or endorsed by the creators or formal training bodies. Skills such as DEARMAN, GIVE, FAST, and Wise Mind appear here for educational use only and can have minor changes.

IFS Information Notice

Internal Family Systems (IFS) was created by Dr. Richard C. Schwartz. This workbook includes simplified IFS concepts to support emotional regulation and self-understanding, but it is not an official IFS program and is not affiliated with, supervised by, or endorsed by the IFS Institute or any formal training bodies.
References to parts work; Managers, Firefighters, Exiles, and Self, are included for educational use and may have been adapted for accessibility.

For any copyright-related enquiries, permissions, or concerns, or if you believe any material has been misused please contact me directly.

References and Inspired Reading

This workbook blends researched frameworks with lived experience and personal interpretation. The following books served as research, information, or simply inspiration:

- Jung, C. G., & Hull, R. F. C. (2023). The Collected Works of CG Jung. In Collected Works of CG Jung
- Linehan, M. M. (2025). DBT skills training manual.
- Linehan, M. M. (2021). Building a life worth living: A memoir.
- McKay, M., Wood, J. C., & Brantley, J. (2019). The dialectical behavior therapy skills workbook: Practical DBT exercises for learning mindfulness, interpersonal effectiveness, emotion regulation, and distress tolerance.
- Wise, S. J. (2022). The Neurodivergent Friendly Workbook of DBT Skills: A Workbook of Dialectial Behaviour Therapy Skills Reframed to be Neurodivergent Friendly with the Added Bonus of Accessible Mindfulness Practices, Sensory Strategies and Managing Meltdowns.
- Schwartz, R. (2021). No bad parts: Healing trauma and restoring wholeness with the internal family systems model.

Copyright © 2025 Bianca McIntyre
All rights reserved. Individual pages may be shared for personal or educational use with credit, without modification, and never for commercial purposes.

Contents

Introduction

- 9 · Where to go
- 11 · Why this book?
- 12 · Why DBT?
- 13 · Why Shadow Work?
- 14 · Why IFS?

Baseline

- 16 · Tools needed
- 17 · Mapping your baseline

Mindfulness

- 22 · What is mindfulness?
- 23 · Why is mindfulness important?
- 24 · What happens when I'm not mindful?
- 25 · What/How skills
- 26 · Mindful myths
- 27 · Awareness exercise
- 28 · Somatic exercise
- 29 · Musical grounding
- 30 · Wise Mind
- 32 · Grounding through senses
- 34 · How skills/ judgement
- 38 · Radical Acceptance
- 42 · Shadow work

Distress Tolerance

- 46 · What happens in the brain?
- 48 · Emotional thermometer
- 49 · TIPP
- 51 · Communicating distress
- 53 · STOP
- 54 · ACCEPTS
- 58 · Self Soothing
- 60 · Radical Acceptance continued
- 62 · Half smile/willing hands
- 64 · Shadow Work

Emotional Regulation

- 68 · What are emotions?
- 69 · Why is emotional regulation important?
- 70 · Expanding your emotional vocabulary
- 72 · Feelings wheel
- 74 · Life filter
- 75 · Checking the facts
- 78 · Opposite Action
- 81 · How to feel your feelings
- 84 · Building a relationship with Self
- 87 · IFS
- 90 · PLEASE
- 92 · Sleep
- 98 · ABC
- 100 · Values
- 104 · Identity pillars
- 107 · Shadow work

Interpersonal Effectiveness

- 110 · Understanding your communication style
- 113 · The 3 C's of connection
- 114 · Boundaries
- 118 · DEARMAN
- 123 · GIVE
- 125 · FAST
- 128 · Shadow work

Integration

- 132 · Moving forward
- 133 · Cheat sheet: Mindfulness
- 135 · Cheat sheet: Distress Tolerance
- 137 · Cheat sheet: Emotional Regulation
- 139 · Cheat sheet Interpersonal Effectiveness
- 141 · Cheat sheet Integration

Where to Go in This Workbook

Use this page whenever you feel lost, overwhelmed, or unsure where to start.

Emotional & Internal States

When everything feels overwhelming:
Distress Tolerance
TIPP • Grounding • Self-soothing • Crisis survival
Helps when emotions spike and you just need to get through the moment.

When your emotions feel confusing or too strong
Emotional Regulation
Name feelings • Opposite Action • PLEASE • Feel Your Feelings
Supports understanding and calming emotional intensity.

When your thoughts won't stop spiralling
Mindfulness
Wise Mind • Curiosity • Observing without judgement
Useful for overthinking, rumination, and disconnection.

When old patterns keep repeating
Shadow Work
Hidden rules • "Why does this bother me?" prompts
Helps you explore shame, triggers, and reactions that feel bigger than the situation.

Relationships & Communication

When communication feels hard
Interpersonal Effectiveness
DEARMAN • GIVE • FAST
Covers asking for what you need, navigating conflict, and staying grounded with others.

When boundaries feel confusing or scary
Boundaries
What I will do • What I won't do • Self-respect.
Helps with people-pleasing, fear of rejection, and holding your own space.

When you feel disconnected from yourself
Meeting Yourself Kindly
Small promises • Curiosity • Reconnection questions
Rebuilds trust, self-respect, and safety within yourself.

Identity, Parts, and Direction

When you feel inner conflict or "multiple versions" of yourself
Internal Family Systems (IFS)
Managers • Firefighters • Exiles • Self
Helps you understand the different parts of you and what they're trying to protect.

When you don't know who you are or what you want
Values & Identity Pillars
Core values • Identity pillars • Living your values
Gives clarity, direction, and motivation for everyday choices.

When you're stuck and don't know where to start
Begin with:
Mindfulness + Emotional Regulation
These two modules make every other skill easier to use.

Why this book?

In a sea of self-help books, I've chosen to throw my own hat in the ring.

This one wasn't written in a burst of inspiration. It was built slowly, over years; years I spent trying to understand my own thoughts, feelings, and behaviours.

In my early twenties, after being diagnosed with **Borderline Personality Disorder** and spending several weeks in and out of the psych ward, I was introduced to **Dialectical Behaviour Therapy (DBT)**; the gold standard for treating emotional dysregulation.
At the time, I wasn't ready for it.
The exercises felt strange, even childish. The structure felt rigid. I couldn't see myself in it, and without that connection, the work didn't land. Not long after, I found myself back in the ward, wondering why nothing seemed to stick.

It took years of trial, error, and self-discovery to realise what was missing.
The missing piece was *me.*

DBT, at its core, is a collection of skills; simple, effective, and sometimes deceptively basic. But imagine I tried to teach you to play guitar when you have no interest in music. You might learn a few chords, but the moment you put it down, the notes fade.
Learning anything new requires interest, and in this case, the "instrument" you're learning is *yourself.*

That's why this workbook is more than DBT exercises.
It's a bridge between theory and self-connection; a space where research-backed skills meet lived experience. It includes journal prompts, reflection pages, and gentle thought exercises designed to help you become curious about your inner world again.

Because most, if not all, of our destructive behaviours are rooted in **shame.**

And we cannot change from a place of shame.

Real change begins with **acceptance**, and acceptance begins with **understanding.**

So as you move through these pages, try to approach yourself with curiosity rather than judgement. Expect moments of discomfort, they're part of growth. But meet them with compassion.

> **How to use this workbook:**
>
> - Move at your own pace. Learning new skills isn't linear. Some ideas will click immediately; others will need time.
> - Engage fully. The more presence you bring to each exercise, the more meaningful the experience becomes.
> - Be kind to yourself. This is a space for learning, not self-criticism.
> - Journal your reflections. Writing helps uncover the beliefs and patterns that often stay hidden.

This isn't a "do it once and be done" kind of book.
It's an ongoing practice; a choice to live differently, to take an active role in your own learning journey, to say; *"I don't want to live this way anymore."*
You'll find space here to write, draw, and reflect. Feel free to add your own pages, to make this workbook a living document of your growth.
So, if you're ready to take an active step toward creating a life worth living, you're in the right place.

Why DBT?

The most common and widely used therapeutic approach in the world today (at the time of writing) is **Cognitive Behavioural Therapy (CBT).**
CBT has earned its reputation because it's effective for many of life's everyday challenges; depression, anxiety, work stress, relationship difficulties, grief. It gives people tools to manage their thoughts and change their behaviours, and for many, it works well enough.

But for those of us with **complex emotional experiences**, CBT can sometimes feel incomplete.
It can feel invalidating, frustrating, and overly focused on "fixing" thoughts instead of understanding emotions. For some, including myself, traditional CBT even made destructive patterns worse, because it taught us to argue with our emotions instead of learning to listen
to them.

One person who also recognised these limitations was **Dr. Marsha Linehan**, the psychologist who created **Dialectical Behaviour Therapy (DBT).**
Her work grew out of her own lived experience of emotional suffering and the struggle to find approaches that truly helped. DBT takes the best parts of CBT; the structure, the practicality, the focus on skill-building, and pairs them with something CBT often lacked: **validation, acceptance, and compassion.**

The word dialectical means *"two opposing truths can exist at the same time."*
In DBT, those truths are:
I accept who I am in this moment.
I want to change who I am in this moment.

That tension is where growth happens.
There can be no change without acceptance.
We cannot change what we refuse to acknowledge, because our brains cannot work with what we deny. If there is nothing to see, there is nothing to transform.

DBT invites us to take an active role in our own lives.
For many of us, our emotions have been driving the car while we're just passengers; reacting, collapsing, or running on autopilot. DBT helps us step into the driver's seat, with four distinct modules that teach the skills and language we need to navigate our inner world.

Most of all, DBT gives us ***hope.***

Hope for those of us who have struggled.
Hope for those who learned to hide their emotions because they felt "too much."
Hope for those who believed that being emotional made them broken.
Hope for those of us who were let down by the system.

Why Shadow Work?

Every person carries parts of themselves that were taught to stay hidden.

The parts that were told to quiet down, toughen up, or fit in. Maybe you learned that anger makes people leave, that sadness makes others uncomfortable, or that being joyful somehow made you "too much." Maybe you were praised for being easy, calm, or unbothered. Or maybe somewhere along the way, you decided that being seen was unsafe.

Over time, you tucked those parts away, thinking it was safer to be easy, agreeable, or invisible.

But the things we bury don't disappear. They show up in the moments that confuse us most; when we overreact, shut down, or judge others without understanding why. Those reactions aren't proof that something is wrong with you; they're reminders of something inside you that still wants to be seen.

The idea of shadow work comes from the psychologist Carl Jung, who believed that every human being carries a "shadow"; the hidden parts of ourselves that we reject, fear, or simply never learned to love. Jung described the shadow not as something bad, but as *something forgotten*. It's the creative child that stopped playing, the angry teenager who never got to speak, the vulnerable adult who learned to mask tenderness behind logic or humour.

Shadow work helps you get curious about those hidden places.

It's an invitation to meet the parts of yourself that once had to hide, and to ask them what they've been trying to protect you from. It's about tracing your reactions back to their roots; to the first time you felt unsafe showing who you were, and gently giving those parts permission to exist again.

The more you listen, the more you realise that your shadows hold valuable information. They tell you what still hurts, what still matters, and what still needs your care. Working with them isn't about fixing yourself. It's about making room for the fullness of who you are; the tender, the fierce, the creative, the scared. *All of it deserving space in your story.*

Through shadow work, you begin to live with a little more honesty, a little less armour, and a lot more peace in knowing that every part of you has always been trying to help you survive.

Why IFS?

Inside every person lives a whole cast of characters; the parts that want to achieve, the parts that want to rest, the ones that worry, and the ones that quietly hold old pain.

Each part has its own voice, its own logic, and its own way of trying to keep you safe. Sometimes they work together beautifully. Other times, they clash, **leaving you caught between feeling too much and feeling nothing at all.**

Internal Family Systems (IFS) was developed by Dr. Richard C. Schwartz, a family therapist who noticed that his clients spoke about their inner experiences the same way families interact; with protectors, rebels, caretakers, and wounded members all trying to be heard. Instead of seeing these parts as problems, Schwartz realised they were personalities within a system, each playing a role to protect the person from pain.

At the centre of this system is **the Self**; calm, compassionate, and steady. The part of you that can listen to all the others without judgement. When you learn to lead your inner world from this place, the noise quiets. The anxious parts can rest, the protective ones soften, and the hurt ones finally feel safe enough to be seen.

IFS offers a way to build a relationship with your inner world rather than trying to control it. It reminds you that every reaction, defence, or shutdown began as an attempt to keep you safe. The perfectionist part that pushes you too hard once protected you from failure. The avoidant part that shuts down during conflict once shielded you from rejection.

When you meet these parts with understanding, your internal system starts to reorganise itself. You begin responding to life from *curiosity instead of crisis*.
And that's what emotional regulation really is; learning to lead yourself with compassion, even when every part of you is fighting for control.

Baseline
made easy

Self Reflection
Tools needed for change

I **ACCEPT** myself completely in this moment

I want to **CHANGE** something about myself

Mindfulness

The practice of intentionally focusing your attention on the present moment, without judgement, to increase self-awareness and emotional clarity

Distress Tolerance

Learning to manage intense emotions or stressful situations without resorting to harmful behaviors, by developing healthier coping strategies and resilience

DBT

Interpersonal Effectiveness

Improving your communication and relationship skills to clearly express your needs, set healthy boundaries, and maintain positive connections with others

Emotional Regulation

Developing skills to recognise, understand, and effectively manage your emotions, allowing for healthier responses and greater emotional stability

+

Shadow Work

Invites us to look at the parts of ourselves we've learned to hide; not to judge or fix them, but to understand how they've been protecting us, so we can bring those parts back into wholeness with compassion and honesty

Internal Family Systems

To help us understand that emotional regulation isn't about silencing parts of ourselves, but about learning to listen to the different voices within us with curiosity and compassion so we can lead from our calm, grounded Self

Mapping your baseline

Before we learn new skills, we learn *ourselves*. This isn't about diagnosing or fixing it's about noticing how you work so change can be intentional, kind, and sustainable.

Emotional regulation is a learning process. Like any language, you need a sense of where you're starting from: your patterns, triggers, body signals, and go-to moves when feelings get big. When you can see your current map, you can choose new routes.

> You're not "bad at feelings." All of us should have been taught these skills as children, unfortunately many of us weren't. They are just skills like learning to talk and learning to walk. Together we can learn this new skill

Why is this exercise important to do?

- We are learning to name our patterns (that we are already aware of) without judgement
- We are bringing awareness to our body's signals before, during, and after emotional spikes
- We are Identifying the needs underneath our reactions
- Starting to build trust in ourselves by choosing one small learning goal to practice this week

What is happening?

In the past few weeks, what situations have created a heightened emotional response? What story are you telling yourself? What are you struggling most with right now?

_____

_____

_____

_____

_____

_____

_____

_____

Mapping your baseline

What story are you telling yourself about those situations?
"When texts slow down, I tell myself I'm being abandoned."

_____

_____

_____

_____

_____

What is your usual response to heightened emotional situations?

What do you do?	**What do you avoid doing?**
(actions, words, tone)	(replying, resting asking for help)

Have you ever noticed how it makes your body feel? Where do you feel it?

_____

_____

_____

_____

Mapping your baseline

What do you think is helping? What do you think is hurting more?

Things that help	Things that hurt
breathing techniques, mindfulness	doomscrolling, avoiding, substances

Important things to remember

- We are simply collecting data, because we cannot change what we don't know we are doing
- We are not trying to be mean to ourselves
- Specific information helps our brain to anchor; "I clench my fists when I'm angry" is easier to work with than "I am all over the place"
- We are not trying to overwhelm our brain, we are trying to better understand the reason behind our behaviours

> We can't change what we can't see, and we don't have to judge what we see to learn from it.

Mindfulness
made easy

Mindfulness

"There's never a good time for Mindfulness, and there's never a bad time. Mindfulness is one of those things you simply do..." - Marsha Linehan

What is Mindfulness?

When you hear the word mindfulness, what do you think of?
Probably a Zen Buddhist monk sitting cross-legged in nature, right?

That's the image most people get, and unfortunately a big part of why many people simply don't try or give up at the first sign of struggle. We compare our beginner efforts to the Olympic standard of mindfulness. Then, when we can't sit still or stop thinking for more than 30 seconds, we assume we're "just not good at it."

Mindfulness is not about perfection or enlightenment. At its core, it's simply practices that help bring you back to the present moment, back into your body, back into the *now*.

Think of Mindfulness as Gym for Your Brain

Imagine it's your first time ever stepping into a gym.
You wouldn't expect yourself to walk in and immediately lift a 50kg weight, right? You'd probably start with a 2kg or 5kg dumbbell, something manageable for where you're at.

> The simple act of training will continuously make your life a little easier

Not being able to lift 50kg doesn't mean you're "not a gym person." It just means your muscles need time to build strength.

Mindfulness works the same way.

lIt's not a trait you either have or don't have, it's a muscle you build through consistent practice. And even if you never reach "Zen Master" status, you'll still develop incredible awareness and emotional strength along the way.

Mindfulness Is the Practice of Noticing

When I say mindfulness, I don't mean sitting in silence for an hour thinking about how bad you are at being mindful.
Mindfulness is simply the practice of noticing.
It's paying attention to what's happening right now, without judging it, without trying to fix it, and without running away from it.

It's not about emptying your mind or forcing peace. It's about awareness. And awareness takes practice.
Continuing the gym metaphor; the more you train your awareness, the easier it becomes to notice when you're spinning out, zoning out, or numbing out.
That's the real power of mindfulness, it creates space.

The space between *reacting* and *responding*.

Mindfulness

Why is Mindfulness Important?

- Reduces stress and suffering by increasing awareness of emotions without reacting impulsively.
- Improves focus and emotional regulation by training the mind to detach from distractions.
- Enhances relationships by being truly present with others.
- Boosts mental well-being by decreasing overthinking, anxiety, and emotional reactivity.

When we're not mindful, we run on autopilot. We react out of habit instead of choice. That's when we scroll for hours, snap at someone we care about, or make decisions that leave us feeling worse later.

Being mindful helps us pause long enough to choose differently. It helps you notice your thoughts before they take over, it helps you notice your emotions before they explode, and notice your body before it burns out.

Mindfulness = noticing without reacting

Mindfulness = being without judgement

Why Is It So Hard?

If you've ever tried to meditate and thought, "I can't do this," you're not broken. Most of us struggle with mindfulness because our nervous systems don't feel safe enough to be still. Often silence can feel suffocating, or make you feel anxious, not peaceful. This is why small steps are necessary, as well as slowly building a relationship with Self.

You're not bad at mindfulness. You're just learning what safety feels like.

Mindfulness

What Happens When I'm Not Mindful?

Our brains are "not mindful" most of the time. Brains are efficient, energy saving machines. It will power down to conserve energy whenever it possibly can. This is why we are able to brush our teeth without thinking, read without paying attention, and even have full conversations with our friends only to realise half way through that we didn't hear anything they said.

How often have you driven to work only to get there not remembering which road you took? It's quite scary to think that we coast through so much of our lives not actually being present, not actually LIVING.

When you're not aware of what's going on inside you, your emotions start running the show. You might zone out, dissociate, or spiral into rumination. You might seek distraction in food, work, your phone, or people who feel familiar but unsafe.

None of this makes you weak. It means your brain is trying to protect you from discomfort.

> **Try this:**
> The next time you catch yourself doom-scrolling or overthinking, pause and ask:
> - What am I trying not to feel right now?
> - What am I trying to create or avoid?
>
> **Awareness is step one. You can't regulate what you don't notice.**

Reflection: Remembering a mindful moment

Think back to the last time you were truly present, even if it was just for a few seconds. It might've been when you were laughing with a friend, feeling the warmth of the sun on your skin, listening to your favourite song, or even taking a deep breath after a long day.
Take a minute to write about it below:
- Where were you?
- What were you doing?
- What did you notice with your senses (what you saw, heard, felt, or smelled)?

_____

_____

_____

_____

Mindfulness

Within the DBT framework we break down mindfulness into two categories;
The **WHAT** skills and the **HOW** skills

Mindfulness WHAT Skills

These are about *what* you do to be mindful.

Observe

Notice what's happening inside and around you.

Your thoughts, sensations, emotions.

Just notice them.

Describe

Put words to what you notice.

"My chest feels tight."
"I'm thinking about work."
"I feel nervous."

Participate

Be fully present in the moment.

Let go of self-consciousness and engage fully in what you're doing.

Mindfulness HOW Skills

These are about *how* you practice mindfulness.

Non-judgementally

Notice what's happening without labeling it good or bad.

judgement adds shame.
Curiosity creates growth.

One-mindfully

Focus on one thing at a time.

If you're eating, eat.

If you're breathing, breathe.

Effectively

Do what works, not what's right or fair.

You can be right and still miserable.

Choose peace instead.

Think of your own real life scenario:

Scenario: You're late for an appointment.

- Observe: "My heart is racing, my stomach's tight."
- Describe: "I'm scared they'll be mad."
- Participate: Take one deep breath before you speak.
- Non-judgementally: "I'm human; sometimes I run late."
- One-mindfully: Focus on parking safely.
- Effectively: Text them you're on your way.

Mindfulness doesn't make life perfect. It helps you meet it as it is.

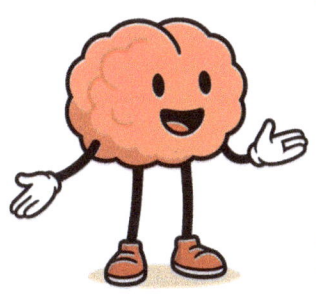

Mindfulness

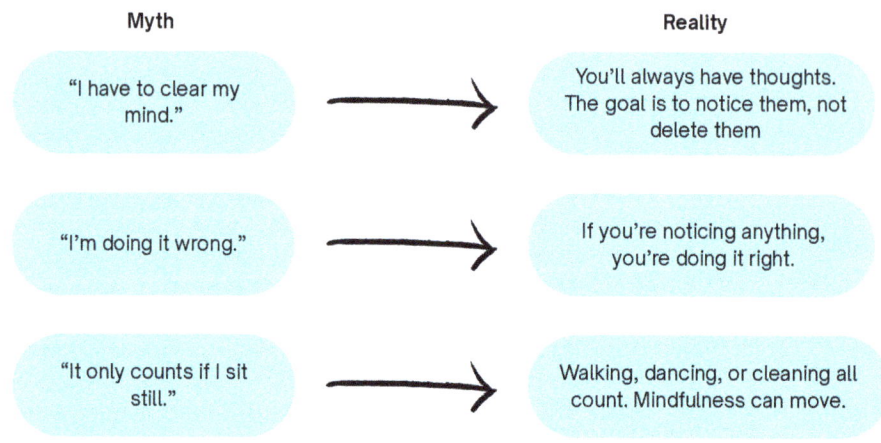

Myth	Reality
"I have to clear my mind."	You'll always have thoughts. The goal is to notice them, not delete them
"I'm doing it wrong."	If you're noticing anything, you're doing it right.
"It only counts if I sit still."	Walking, dancing, or cleaning all count. Mindfulness can move.

Mindfulness is not about being still. It's about being present. It's about teaching your brain recall.

One way to think about this is to imagine your brain as a puppy. When you first bring the puppy home, it doesn't know its name. You spend time patiently teaching it, repeating the same cue over and over. At first, the puppy doesn't even look up. After a few training sessions, it starts to respond occasionally, glancing at you before running back to whatever it was doing. With consistency and practice, the puppy learns that when you call its name, it's time to come back.

Your brain works the same way. Mindfulness is the training that helps your brain learn to "*come when you call.*" And just like a puppy, your mind will often find more interesting things to chase. Things like distractions, daydreams, anxiety, or anything that pulls it away from the present moment. Your brain prefers to conserve energy, so it will resist at first. But with gentle repetition, it learns. Over time, it begins to return to you more easily, staying with you a little longer each time.

Reflection: Training Your Mind Like a Puppy

Notice how many times your mind wanders today.
Each time it does, gently call it back, the same way you'd call a puppy you love.

What helps your attention "come when you call"?

_____

_____

The goal is allowing your mind to wander, and then to practice bringing it home.

Mindfulness

Let these practices become part of your day in a way that feels natural.

Approach every exercise with curiosity and understanding, not judgement.

Your brain will resist change, that's normal. If something feels too difficult, pause and come back to it later. Learning these skills takes time. It's not about getting it right overnight but building awareness over a lifetime.

Awareness Exercise

Awareness is one of the most powerful tools we have.
To understand how it works, try this simple exercise:

Step 1: Without changing your current position, bring your attention to the bottoms of your feet.
Don't move them. Don't touch them. Just think about them.

Step 2: Imagine sending warm air to the soles of your feet.

Step 3: After a little while, you might notice tingling, warmth, or a subtle shift in sensation. That's your body responding to your awareness.

You can repeat this with any part of your body; your hands, shoulders, or face.

Try slowly moving your awareness from one area to another, noticing what changes.

Reflection

Now take a moment to describe what you noticed:

- What did you feel in your body?
- Did anything shift when you focused on it?
- How did it feel to slow down and pay attention?

_____

_____

_____

It might not feel the same every time, and sometimes you might not feel much at all. The goal is simply to notice what's happening right now.

Mindfulness

> **Connecting the Practice**
>
> In this short exercise, you've practiced three of the **"What"** skills from mindfulness:
>
> **Observe:** Noticing your body without trying to change it.
> **Describe:** Putting your experience into words.
> **Participate:** Fully engaging in the moment.

Mindfulness Isn't Just Mental. It's Physical

Your body tells the truth even when your mind doesn't want to listen.
It holds tension, emotion, and memories that we've learned to push aside, distract from, or pretend aren't there.

When we talk about mindfulness, it's not enough to sit and think about being calm, because you can't think your way into safety.

Your body stores what your mind avoids.
Maybe you've noticed this before: the tight chest when you're anxious, the lump in your throat when you're trying not to cry, the ache in your shoulders after holding everything together all day. These aren't random sensations. They're your body trying to talk to you.
Mindfulness is how we start listening again.
It isn't about forcing stillness or having a quiet mind. It's about coming home to your body. Feeling what's there without trying to change it. When you reconnect with your physical sensations, you give your nervous system permission to slow down, to breathe, and to feel safe again.

You don't need to meditate on a mountain or light a candle for this. You can start right where you are, using movement, breath, and sensory awareness to get out of your head and back into your body.

Simple Somatic Exercises

- Shake it out. Shake your hands, arms, or legs for 30 seconds. Let yourself be a little silly. Notice the tingling or warmth that follows. That's your body releasing stored energy.
- Hum or sing. Put on a favourite song and hum along. Feel the vibration in your chest and throat. That gentle buzz stimulates your vagus nerve, the body's natural calming system.
- Tap your chest gently while breathing out slowly. Feel the rhythm under your hand. Let each exhale get a little longer and a little softer.
- Go barefoot. Step outside or onto your floor and notice what's under your feet. The temperature, the texture, the pressure. Let your attention rest there.
- Let your body move. Play music and let your body sway, stretch, or dance. Don't think about how it looks. Focus on how it feels to move freely.

There's no right way to do this. Just notice what feels grounding for you. Some days that might be a walk, other days it might be singing in the car or lying still with your hand on your chest.

Your body is always communicating. Mindfulness is simply the practice of remembering to listen.

Mindfulness

Musical Grounding

Step 1: Pick one song you like preferably one with a rhythm you can feel.
Step 2: Listen with your whole body. No multitasking, no scrolling.
Step 3: Notice how your body wants to move. Let it.

If music feels overstimulating, try humming softly instead. The vibration itself stimulates your vagus nerve.

> **Why does this work?**
> When your body moves, hums, or connects with your senses, you're signalling safety to your brain. This activates the parasympathetic nervous system, the part that slows your heart rate, deepens your breath, and helps you feel grounded again.

Reflection

Now take a moment to describe what you noticed:

- What sensations did you notice most strongly?
- Did anything shift in your breathing or posture?
- What felt awkward, relaxing, or surprising?

> Each time you practice, you strengthen your ability to stay present in your body and respond with awareness instead of autopilot.

_____

_____

_____

Personalise Your Experience

- What are some mindful aspects you can easily add to your daily practice that have not been mentioned?
- Or how can you modify the ones that have been mentioned to better fit into your life?

_____

_____

_____

_____

Mindfulness

Wise Mind is the quiet voice underneath both panic and logic. It's the space that says: I hear both sides, and I'll choose what **helps me most**.

What is Wise Mind?

Wise Mind is one of the core DBT skills. It's the balance between two extremes; **Emotion Mind** (impulsive, reactive, driven by feelings) and **Rational Mind** (detached, cold, focused only on logic).
Wise Mind isn't about perfection or neutrality. It's about integrating both truth and feeling; letting your emotional intuition and your logical reasoning coexist.
In practice, Wise Mind feels like an inner knowing. That quiet gut feeling that says, "This makes sense and it also feels right."

Examples:

Emotion Mind:
You argue with a loved one and lash out. You say things to hurt them because you feel hurt. Afterwards, shame and isolation follow.

Rational Mind:
You shut down, retreat into logic, list facts, and avoid emotions altogether. You "win" the argument but lose connection.

Wise Mind:
You pause before reacting. You notice what you feel and what the other person might be feeling. You express yourself calmly, own your part, and focus on repair rather than being right.

Wise Mind doesn't mean you always stay calm. It means you know how to return to calm more quickly.

How to Access Wise Mind

- Pause before reacting.
- Breathe or ground yourself. Feel your feet, count your breaths, use temperature or sound.
- Check both sides: What are my emotions saying? What are the facts saying?
- Ask: What action honours both truth and feeling?

Wise Mind often feels like an unreachable middle ground between emotional storms and overthinking spirals.
Stillness can feel unnatural. The key is movement and sensory grounding: walk, rock, hum, or press your hands together.

That's how your body finds regulation first, your mind follows after.

Mindfulness

Reflecting on Your Three Minds

Think back to a time when your emotions took over.

- What did you feel in your body?
- How did you react?
- What was the outcome?

_____

_____

_____

Think of a time you shut your emotions off and stayed in logic.

- What did you gain?
- What did you lose?

_____

_____

Think of a time you balanced both.

- How did you know what to do?
- What did that feel like in your body?

_____

_____

Living From Wise Mind

Wise Mind isn't just for conflict. It's a way of living "the middle path", noticing when you're swinging too far toward doing or too far toward being.

Too much doing looks like burnout.
Too much being looks like paralysis.
Wise Mind finds rhythm between the two.

Start with one mindful activity a day:

- Brush your teeth and notice every movement.
- Cook and pay attention to the colours, textures, smells.
- Shower and focus on the water's temperature.

These small moments build self-trust, the foundation of Wise Mind.

Mindfulness

Now that we have a better understanding of the purpose of building **awareness** and developing a stronger **Wise Mind**. Here are some more easy mindfulness exercises to incorporate

Grounding through senses

At any point during the day, take a moment to experience the world through your senses.

Sight

Observe using your sight: What can you see? Can you see different colours? Can you see different textures? Can you switch between moving your sight from close up to far away?

Smell

Observe using your smell: Pick something you like the smell of like a candle or perfume. Can you smell the different aspects of the object? Is it sweet? Is it spicy? Is it earthy?

Taste

Observe using your taste: Use an easy to hold food item like candy or a fruit. Bring awareness to the sensations in your mouth. Is it sweet? Is it difficult to chew?

Touch

Observe using your hearing: What are some sounds in the environment? Can you hear your own breathing? Can you switch between listening to sounds close by to hearing things far away?

Sound

Observe using your touch: Choose an object that you can pick up. Examine the object with your touch, is it rough? Is it smooth? Is it heavy? Is it light?

Mindfulness

Mindfulness isn't just noticing what's happening. It's asking, **"Why?"** without judgement.

A key part of building new skills is taking time to reflect and understand.

Learning the skill itself is only half the process. The other half is being curious enough about ourselves to want to change.

Many of our painful or self-destructive behaviours come from shame. Shame is a deeply rooted emotion that makes us feel separate or rejected from others. It convinces us that we are unworthy of connection or care.

Living in that mindset for too long can make us give our power away. It keeps us trapped in cycles of pity and helplessness.

If I am bad, then what's the point? Bad things will always happen to me. The world is against me. Sound familiar?

People often compare guilt and shame.
Guilt says, "I've done something wrong."
Shame says, "I am something wrong."

To grow, we have to step out of that story. The way out of *shame* is through *understanding*.

And the quickest way to understanding is *curiosity*.

To get out of **SHAME**

We need **UNDERSTANDING**

Which is gained through **CURIOSITY**

When you approach life with curiosity instead of expectation, you are presented with opportunities instead of problems.

Curiosity allows us to explore why we do what we do, instead of forcing ourselves to be different. It helps us approach every moment, even painful ones, with understanding and acceptance rather than self-hatred and disappointment.

Try noticing the difference between these two approaches:

Expectation: "I have to fix this."
Curiosity: "I wonder why this matters so much to me."

Expectation pushes us toward *performance* and *perfection*.
Curiosity leads us toward *awareness*, *compassion*, and *real growth*.

Mindfulness
Judgement, the inner self, and our **HOW** skills

Beginning with Curiosity

Where do we begin with curiosity?
By building a relationship with ourselves that is free from unrealistic expectations.
One powerful way to do this is through **Shadow Work**, a concept introduced by psychologist Carl Jung. Jung explained that each of us carries traits, emotions, and aspects of ourselves that we've learned to suppress. He called this our *shadow self*.

Your shadow self isn't just made up of the "negative" parts of you. It can also hold your creativity, freedom, confidence, and self-expression, parts of you that have been hidden or silenced.

Why do we suppress these parts?

Because somewhere along the way, we were taught they were shameful or wrong.
Maybe your family mocked you for dressing a certain way.
Maybe your peers only praised one side of your personality, so you learned to *hide* the rest.
We often see this pattern in people who get angry or uncomfortable with the self-expression of others.
If I have subconsciously told myself I'm not allowed to express who I am, then I'll often hold others to that same rule without realising it.

Awareness and the HOW Skills

This is where the **HOW** mindfulness skills become important.
The first step in building a genuine relationship with yourself is becoming aware of who you are and what you've been trying to suppress.

Judgement plays a big role here. Many people think the goal is to replace negative judgements with positive ones, but the real skill is to approach things without judgement at all.
Judgement comes from black-and-white thinking, the "either/or" mindset where we idealise or devalue, label or categorise.

When we judge someone, there are only two participants in that comparison: us and them. Even when the judgement sounds positive, it still creates a competition or hierarchy. Someone always ends up being "better" or "worse."

So, what exactly is a judgement, and how is it different from simply having an opinion?

A judgement is an **opinion** that carries heavy emotional weight and *moral criticism*.
It often hides behind words like good, bad, right, wrong, should, or shouldn't.

Judgements constantly place people into moral competitions they never agreed to join.

Mindfulness

Reflection: Noticing Judgements in Everyday Life

Judgement is often automatic. It slips into our thoughts before we even notice it's there.

The goal isn't to get rid of judgement entirely but to start recognising when it shows up and how it feels in your body and mind.

Take a moment to reflect:

- What kinds of things or people do I tend to judge most often?
- What emotion usually comes with that judgement? Frustration, jealousy, shame, superiority?
- What might this judgement be protecting me from feeling or acknowledging?
- How would it feel to replace that judgement with curiosity?

Curiosity doesn't mean agreeing with everything. It means staying open long enough to understand.

_____

_____

_____

_____

Now, try paying attention to your thoughts over the next 24 hours.

Each time you notice yourself judging someone (including yourself), pause and ask:

"What story am I telling myself right now?"
"What would it look like to see this moment without labels?"

Write down any insights that come up below.

_____

_____

_____

_____

Judgement closes. Curiosity opens. Each time you choose to understand instead of criticise, you build a kinder relationship with yourself and the world around you.

Mindfulness

Reflection in Practice: Understanding Judgement

You're going about your day when you notice someone dressed very eccentrically.
Your heart picks up, your skin tingles, and before you even think about it, the thought appears:

"Wow, what an absolute clown. Why would they wear something like that? I'd never do that, it's so wrong and stupid."

Now, **pause**.
Notice the difference between saying;

"I don't like what that person is wearing," and *"What that person is wearing is wrong and awful."*

One is preference. The other is *judgement*.
Take a moment to ask yourself:

- What story am I telling myself here?
- Where did I learn that dressing that way is wrong?

Your mind might reply with thoughts like:

"They just want attention."
"They're trying too hard."
"They just want to be seen."

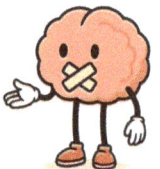

What "rules" do we unconsciously hold about how people should behave, dress, or express themselves?

Then, take it one step deeper:

- Why do I believe that wanting attention or being seen is bad?

Maybe you were told you were "too loud" or "too much" as a child.
Maybe you were punished for standing out or expressing yourself boldly.
Maybe you were praised for being the quiet one, the easy child who learned that blending in was safest.

Without realising it, we all carry invisible "shadow rules", the ones we learned growing up about what is acceptable and what isn't.
When someone's behaviour makes us uncomfortable, it often means they've broken one of those hidden rules we didn't even know we were following.
Becoming aware of these rules doesn't mean you'll suddenly love what used to bother you.
It simply gives you choice; *the power to respond consciously instead of reacting automatically.*
Maybe you'll soften those old rules, allowing a little more freedom or expression in yourself.
Or maybe you'll still think, "That outfit isn't for me," and continue with your day; calm, grounded, and self-aware.
Either way, you'll have saved yourself from the unnecessary spike of judgement, shame, and stress that comes from old stories you no longer
need to live by.

Mindfulness

Releasing Judgement, Embracing Curiosity

Judgement is one of the mind's quickest ways to regain control. It sorts people, experiences, and emotions into "good" or "bad."

The problem is that judgement removes nuance. It disconnects us from empathy, both for ourselves and others.
Many people try to go from negative judgement to positive judgement, but both are still judgement.

Judgement	Understanding
"They shouldn't be so emotional."	"They're expressing something I've learned to hide

The goal is understanding without evaluation. Judgement keeps us in comparison.
Understanding keeps us in connection.

Practice: The Judgement Journal

For one day, notice every judgement that crosses your mind; toward others, yourself, your body, your thoughts.

Write them down, then rewrite each one with curiosity:

Judgement	Curious Reframe
I'm so lazy	What does my body need right now?
I shouldn't feel this way	What is this feeling trying to tell me?

Over time, you'll notice how judgement loses its charge when replaced with understanding.

Mindfulness

This brings us to one of the most important concepts in DBT and mindfulness; *Radical Acceptance*.

> Radical Acceptance is the ability to completely accept your current reality as it is, without judgement.

It sounds simple, but it's one of the hardest skills to practice. To understand it fully, it helps to start with what Radical Acceptance is not.

Radical Acceptance is Not:

- Liking your current reality.
- Approving or condoning what's happening.
- Becoming a doormat or letting people mistreat you.
- Avoiding accountability or giving up on change.

Radical Acceptance simply means acknowledging, "Whatever is happening right now, whether I like it or not, is my reality."

From this place of awareness, you can decide what, if anything, is within your control to change.

Why Radical Acceptance Matters

Practicing Radical Acceptance helps to:

- Reduce unnecessary emotional pain and suffering.
- Free you from the past and allow emotional healing.
- Create space for productive action instead of reactive behaviour.
- Strengthen mindfulness and effective problem-solving.
- Encourage self-compassion and resilience.
- Release the weight of "should've" and "could've."

Pain is an inevitable part of life. The goal of Radical Acceptance isn't to deny or avoid this truth. It isn't pretending that painful experiences won't happen. It's understanding that life WILL be painful but dwelling on it will prolong suffering. Instead, it's about facing life fully, the joy and the pain, and meeting it with awareness instead of resistance.

When we accept reality, we stop fighting the facts. This doesn't mean we become passive. It means we stop wasting energy on what we can't change and use that energy to take action where we can.

Ultimately, we can either see life as something that happens to us, or we can take an active role by accepting what is and choosing how to respond.

Mindfulness

Steps to Practice Radical Acceptance

Notice When You're Fighting Reality

The first step in changing any pattern of thinking or behaviour is simple acknowledgement.
We can't change what we don't recognise.
Bring gentle attention to your situation and your thoughts.
Clearly describe what you're struggling to accept, without exaggerating or minimising it.

It's surprisingly easy to resist reality without realising it, especially if you've been avoiding a situation or distracting yourself from it.

Recognising that you're stuck in non-acceptance is often the most powerful first step toward actually accepting reality.

Stick to the facts. Leave out the judgement.

Remind Yourself That Reality Is Exactly What It Is

Sometimes acceptance begins with the simplest reminders.
You might quietly tell yourself:

"It is what it is."
"Reality just is."
"This situation simply exists."

These statements may feel flat or frustrating at first, but they help you release the urge to argue with reality. They bring you closer to awareness, where acceptance becomes possible.

Understanding is not approval.

Explore What Led to This Reality

Acceptance often becomes easier when you understand how and why a situation came to be.
People sometimes resist looking deeper because they worry it means excusing harmful behaviour. But understanding a cause isn't about making excuses, it's about gaining clarity.

You can still hold yourself or others accountable while exploring what contributed to the situation.

Reflect on these questions:
- When have I resisted exploring causes because it felt like giving excuses?
- When have others resisted understanding my behaviour for the same reason?

Mindfulness

Practice Accepting with Mind, Body, and Spirit

Acceptance can start begrudgingly. Radical Acceptance means embracing reality fully, not halfway, and without judgement.

Begin by intentionally letting go.

Notice any physical tension. This is your body's way of showing resistance.
Take a breath, soften your shoulders, unclench your jaw, and allow yourself to release the tightness.
If your mind pushes back with thoughts like, "I don't want this," that's normal.
Take another slow breath. Relax again. Keep practicing letting go.
You can use mindfulness techniques to stay grounded in the present moment, focusing on your breath, body, or senses.

Each time you return to awareness, you strengthen your ability to accept reality as it is.

Acceptance doesn't erase pain. It helps you stop adding to it.

Reflection: Practicing Acceptance

Think of a situation in your life that you've struggled to accept.
Use the space below to describe it without judgement or story. Then reflect on what might change if you stopped fighting it.

_____

_____

_____

_____

_____

_____

_____

Mindfulness

Accepting Yourself

Radical Acceptance also includes accepting *yourself*, both physically and mentally.

Accepting who you are, imperfections and all, can feel like the hardest part. It takes time, effort, and practice, especially if you've spent years resisting or criticising yourself. When we don't accept ourselves, we create constant tension, frustration, and grief.
Real acceptance is not a single moment; it's a repeated act of turning your mind toward compassion again and again.
When you're struggling emotionally, feeling anxious, overwhelmed, or low, acceptance means noticing your thoughts without being consumed by them.

You might say to yourself:
"I'm having this thought right now."

Then gently bring your attention back to the present. You may need to do this many times before it feels natural, and that's okay.

Radical Acceptance of Self

Try this:

Take a few moments to reflect on the parts of yourself that you find hardest to accept. As you do, allow whatever emotions come up to simply exist. Don't push them away.
Begin by noticing the aspects of yourself that cause sadness, frustration, or discomfort. With those in mind, repeat the following phrases, either quietly or out loud, as you practice self-acceptance:

"I don't have to like every part of myself to accept who I am completely."

"My imperfections and struggles don't define my worth; they make me human."

"Even though this part of me is difficult, it deserves compassion, not rejection."

"Resisting who I am only prolongs my suffering. Acceptance frees me to grow."

"I choose to accept myself exactly as I am in this moment, knowing acceptance is the first step toward change."

Add your own:

_____

_____

_____

Shadow Work

Mindfulness invites you to meet yourself with honesty. It's the practice of noticing what's happening inside you, the thoughts, sensations, and emotions that usually slip by unnoticed. These reflections are a space to slow down and listen to the quieter parts of yourself: the ones that speak through tension in your shoulders, a sudden sigh, or the urge to reach for distraction.

- When my mind drifts, where does it tend to go? What might that be trying to show me?

___

___

___

___

- What emotions or memories do I avoid sitting with, and what do I fear might happen if I did?

___

___

___

___

- How do I speak to myself when I make a mistake? What tone do I use?

___

___

___

___

Shadow Work

- What would it feel like to give myself the same patience I give others?

- When do I find myself mentally checked out, distracted, or disconnected? What emotions am I avoiding in those moments?

- What thoughts tend to pull me away from the present moment? Can I notice any patterns or triggers behind this?

Distress Tolerance
made easy

Distress Tolerance

Distress Tolerance is about learning how to cope when emotions feel too big, too sudden, or too painful to manage. These skills help you survive intense emotional waves without reacting impulsively or doing something that might make things worse.

The goal isn't to erase pain or discomfort. It's to stay grounded, calm, and clear enough to make choices that don't cause more harm. These tools help you hold steady until the emotional storm passes.

But before we talk about the skills, it's important to understand why our brain sometimes takes over and why emotional crises can feel so out of control.

You can't stop the waves, but you can learn to surf them.

What Happens in the Brain

When something "triggers" you, it means your amygdala has been activated. The amygdala is your emotional brain. Its job is to scan for danger and keep you safe. It controls emotional responses like fear, anger, and anxiety.
The problem is that this system hasn't evolved much since prehistoric times.
Back then, it protected us from real threats, like predators.

Today, our stressors are different: emails, deadlines, arguments, social rejection.

Even though the threats have changed, our brain still reacts as if we're being chased by a lion.

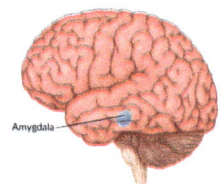

Amygdala;
behaviour brain, responsible for fight, flight, freeze, fawn

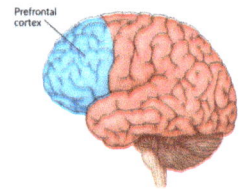

Prefrontal cortex;
logic brain, responsible for reasoning, consequences

When the amygdala detects danger, it activates the fear response, often called fight, flight, freeze, or fawn.

At the same time, the prefrontal cortex, which is the rational, problem-solving part of the brain, temporarily "shuts down."

This would've been beneficial in prehistoric times because there is no time to reason with a lion, so there is no need for logic or communication, there is only time for survival.

That's why, in moments of panic or rage, logic goes out the window. Your brain's priority is survival, not reason.

Distress Tolerance

"By refusing to accept the misery that it takes to climb out of hell, you end up falling back into hell repeatedly, only to have to start over and over again," - Marsha Linehan

The Modern Problem

Your brain's main priority during stress is survival. It doesn't care whether the threat is physical or emotional; it only knows something feels unsafe.

The problem is that most modern stressors aren't life-threatening. Yet our body still reacts as though they are. The same system that once helped us escape predators now activates during arguments, deadlines, or emotional rejection. This mismatch can create unnecessary suffering.
Our body goes into full survival mode when what we really need is connection, communication, or rest.

Learning distress tolerance skills helps bridge this gap, teaching the body that not every discomfort is danger, and that safety can be found again, even in the middle of strong emotion.

Getting the Thinking Brain Back Online

When your fear response takes over, your thinking brain temporarily goes offline. The good news is, you can bring it back.

There are two reliable ways to do this:

- Changing your body temperature
- Changing your heart rate

In the following pages, you'll explore techniques that use both methods to help calm your nervous system and restore balance.

You'll also learn how to choose the right distress tolerance skill depending on the level of intensity you're experiencing.

Reflection: Understanding Your Reactions

Think back to a time when you felt completely overwhelmed or reactive.

- What triggered you?
- How did your body feel in that moment?
- Looking back, what might your brain have been trying to protect you from?

_____

_____

_____

Distress Tolerance

Preparing to Use Distress Tolerance Skills

Distress tolerance works best when you don't wait for the crisis to hit before deciding what to do. When you start paying attention to your patterns, you begin to see that emotional intensity isn't a rare event you "shouldn't" have; it's simply part of being human. Because of that, preparation becomes an act of care. When you start taking an active role in your life and approach your behaviour with curiosity instead of expectation, you begin to realise that it's not *if* you'll experience heightened emotions, it's **when**.

> Emotional intensity is part of being human.

By building small habits and becoming familiar with your tools, your brain learns where to reach when things feel overwhelming. The more these skills live in your daily life, the easier it is to lean on them when it matters.
Some skills are most effective when your emotions are only rising a little, while others are designed for moments that feel more like a surge.

To figure out which tool fits the moment, it can help to use an inner emotional thermometer; a simple way of checking in with how intensely everything feels inside your body.
Instead of trying to measure your feelings precisely, you're simply noticing your internal temperature:

- What does my body feel like right now?
- How strong is the pull to react or shut down?
- Do I need grounding, soothing, distraction, or something that helps me problem-solve?

The goal isn't to rate yourself perfectly. It's to understand the difference between "I feel activated,"

"I feel overwhelmed," and "I feel like I'm losing control," so you aren't guessing which skill might help.

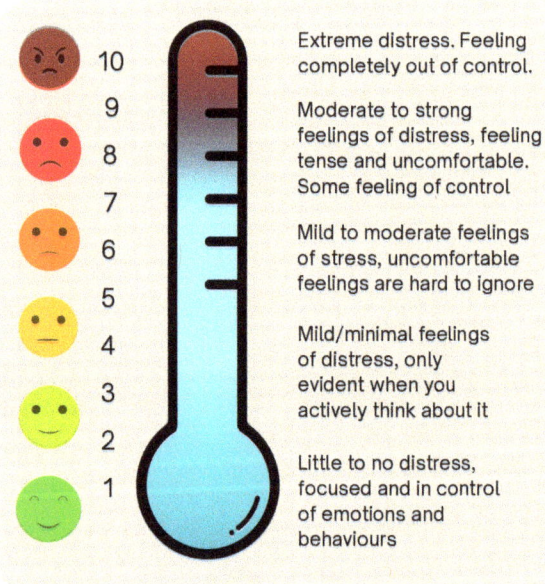

10 — Extreme distress. Feeling completely out of control.

9, 8 — Moderate to strong feelings of distress, feeling tense and uncomfortable. Some feeling of control

7, 6 — Mild to moderate feelings of stress, uncomfortable feelings are hard to ignore

5, 4 — Mild/minimal feelings of distress, only evident when you actively think about it

3, 2, 1 — Little to no distress, focused and in control of emotions and behaviours

The more you learn your internal signals, the more confident you become in supporting yourself through emotional waves.

Willingness	Radical Acceptance		Self Soothing		Accepts		STOP		TIPP
1	2	3	4	5	6	7	8	9	10

The goal isn't perfection; it's learning which tools are realistic for you in different emotional states.

Distress Tolerance

When emotions reach their peak, logic usually goes offline. You can't reason your way out of an emotional crisis when your nervous system is flooded. The **TIPP** skill is designed to help you calm your body first so that your thinking brain can come back online.
Each part works to regulate your body's stress response and lower emotional intensity quickly.

T.I.P.P skill

Changing your body temperature can activate your body's calming system almost instantly.

Things to try:
Splash your face with cold water. Run cold water over your wrists. Have a cold shower. Hold something cold against your chest or the sides of your neck. Activate your mammalian reflex* by dunking your face into a bowl of cold water, passing your temples, while holding your breath. Hold a cold towel over your face. Keep an ice cube wrapped in cloth in your hands.

When your body floods with adrenaline, it needs a release.
Invigorating your body through movement helps burn off that energy and stimulate your nervous system.

Try moving your body in any way that feels accessible, brisk walking, dancing to a song, stretching, or shaking out your arms. You don't need to aim for intensity or perfection; the goal is simply to move energy through the body.
This physical movement helps clear stress hormones, stabilises your heart rate, and brings a sense of relief.

Once your body begins to settle, focus on your breath.
Slow, rhythmic breathing balances your heart rate and helps the nervous system recognise safety again.

Things to try:
- Breathing in for 4 seconds, holding for 1, and breathing out for 6.
- Keep your focus on the exhale, the longer out-breath activates your body's relaxation response.
- Breathe in for 4, hold for 4, out for 4, hold for 4.
- Breathe in once, without breathing out breathe in again, hold for 2, breathe out all your air.

Finally, release any lingering tension in your body by mindfully combining breathing and tensing your muscles.

Tense a muscle group as you inhale, then relax it fully as you exhale. Move through your body; face, shoulders, hands, legs. Notice how relaxation feels.
This practice retrains your body to recognise calm, even in moments of discomfort.

*Using cold water to trigger the dive reflex quickly lowers heart rate. Individuals with heart issues, eating disorders, or slow heart rates should consult a medical provider first.

Distress Tolerance

After trying the TIPP steps, take a few moments to reflect:

- Which step felt most effective for you?
- What sensations did you notice as your body calmed down?
- How could you include one of these steps in your daily routine?

_____

_____

Preparation Plan

Things I need to buy/prepare (eg: bowl for water, towel in fridge, ice)

_____

_____

Exercises I could do

_____

_____

Things I need to coordinate with my loved ones

_____

_____

Think of it like emotional first aid: you can't build the kit during the emergency.

Distress Tolerance

Communicating During Distress

Distressful experiences can happen at any time, and often the people closest to us are directly or indirectly involved. This is why it helps to involve our loved ones in our emotional regulation journey whenever possible.

Think back to a time when you had a strong emotional reaction around someone you care about. In that moment, it's almost impossible to calmly say, "I'm really overwhelmed right now, please give me some space," or "I know it doesn't look like it, but what I need right now is a hug."
This isn't because you lack communication skills. It's because those statements require your thinking brain and, as we now know, when your amygdala is activated, your prefrontal cortex (the rational part of your brain) goes offline. In other words, your body is in survival mode.

What Can We Do Instead?

One simple and effective strategy is to use code words with the people you trust.
When you pre-plan these words together, they become an easy shorthand for expressing what you need in moments when words are hard to find.

> Because sometimes saying "**WATERMELON**" is a lot easier than trying to explain "I'm triggered, and I need a hug."

How to Create Your Code Words

This system only works if it's discussed and agreed upon beforehand. It also takes time to learn what you actually need when you're triggered.
Think back to a recent or past emotional episode and reflect on what would have helped in that moment.

For example:

"If I get triggered and have passed the point of no return, I'll say 'watermelon', that means I need you to hug me even if I look angry or distant."

"If I get triggered and I say 'balloon,' it means I need space to cool down before I say something I regret."

Take time to identify what your emotional triggers are and the kind of support that feels grounding for you. Then, clearly communicate that with the people in your life.

Support works best when everyone knows the rules.

Distress Tolerance

Shared Responsibility

While it's important to create a supportive environment, it's equally important to take responsibility for your own emotional regulation.

This means:

- Recognising your triggers.
- Accepting your emotions without shame.
- Communicating your needs as clearly as you can.
- Taking accountability for your actions and repairs afterward.

When both you and your loved ones understand how to respond to distress, you create safety; not just within yourself, but within your relationships too.

Reflection: Creating Your Support System

- What are some of your emotional triggers?
- What kind of support helps you most when you feel overwhelmed?
- What code word or signal could you use to express those needs easily?

_____

_____

_____

_____

_____

_____

_____

_____

Distress Tolerance

Getting your thinking brain back online is a big step, but it doesn't mean you're suddenly calm or that the emotion disappears.
You may still feel angry, sad, or distressed, the difference is that now you have enough control to choose what happens next.
The STOP skill is designed to help you pause before reacting, giving you space to respond in a way that reflects your values instead of your impulses. It's a grounding tool that helps bridge the gap between emotion and action.

STOP

The moment you notice your distress rising, stop, and notice

Freeze the action, the conversation, or the behaviour.
Pausing interrupts impulsive reactions, giving you control instead of emotions driving your decisions.
The more we practice mindfulness, the easier this step will become.

TAKE A STEP

Give yourself a little distance; physically, mentally, or both.

Take a breath, step away from the situation if possible, or visualise yourself zooming out.
This small separation helps reduce the intensity of the moment and gives your mind a chance to settle and gain perspective.

OBSERVE

Bring awareness to what's happening, both inside and around you.

Notice what triggered you, what you're feeling in your body, and what thoughts are running through your mind.
You're not analysing or judging, just observing.

PROCEED

Once you've stopped, stepped back, and observed, you're ready to act, but with awareness.both inside and around you.

Ask yourself:
- What outcome do I want from this situation?
- What action will help me move closer to that?
- What would be the most effective way to respond right now?

Then move forward with intention, not impulse.

Between the emotion and the action, there is a pause, and in that pause lies your power.

Distress Tolerance

The ACCEPTS Skill

Sometimes we need to remind ourselves that the brain doesn't always tell the truth. When emotions are intense, they can convince us they'll last forever, but emotions aren't permanent. Their purpose is to show up, be felt, and then pass.

Trying to think your way through strong emotions rarely works. Instead, DBT uses a "body-up" approach, where you act first and let your emotions follow.
Your brain works a lot like a computer: it runs whatever program you feed it.
That's why skills like ACCEPTS and Opposite Action are so powerful.
When you deliberately engage in behaviours that contradict how you feel, your brain adjusts by creating emotions that match your new actions.

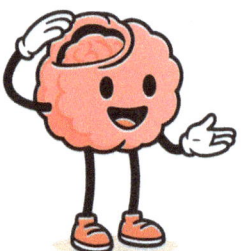

Keep in mind that these skills don't erase problems, they simply give you space to ride the emotional wave without being swept away.

Why We Use Distraction Skills

When emotions are at their peak, thinking clearly isn't possible. Trying to solve problems in that state usually makes things worse.

Distraction skills like ACCEPTS give your brain the time it needs to settle before re-engaging with what's hard.

This isn't avoidance, it's creating space for perspective.
Once your distress comes down, *you can return to the situation with clarity and choice*.

Distraction isn't running away. It's taking a pause so you can come back stronger.

Body-Up Approach

When we're distressed, our brain's emotional centre runs the show. Logical reasoning takes a back seat.
By taking action first, by moving, distracting, or doing something purposeful we shift our body's chemistry.

This allows our emotions to catch up with our actions.
The body moves first, the feelings follow.

Distress Tolerance

ACCEPTS is a skill for when emotions are too high for logic, but not high enough for crisis interventions like TIPP.
Think of it as your middle-ground skill, the one you reach for when you need to ride out emotional discomfort safely.

Do something that keeps you fully engaged in the present moment.
It doesn't need to fix the problem; it just helps shift your attention long enough for your mind to calm.

Try activities that use your one-mindfully skill: cooking, painting, cleaning, gaming, or walking outside. The goal is presence, not productivity.

Helping others can feel hard when you're in distress, and that's exactly why it works. Turning your focus outward interrupts the loop of self-criticism and reconnects you to purpose.

If you're struggling, start small: message a friend, offer to help someone run an errand, or donate clothes you no longer need.
Even tiny acts of contribution remind your brain that you still have value and agency.

This isn't about comparing yourself to others. It's about remembering your own strength.

Think back to a time when things felt unbearable. How did you get through it? How long did it take for the emotion to ease?
Use that memory as proof that what feels endless right now will also pass.

This skill is about shifting or validating how you feel.

If you're sad, listening to sad music might help you feel understood.
Or you can try the opposite, watch a funny video, dance, or do something playful.
Both are valid approaches. One helps you process, the other helps you redirect.
Either way, you're engaging with your emotion instead of avoiding it.

Distress Tolerance

Sometimes you need a mental break from your thoughts before you can face them.

Imagine putting your distressing thought or problem into a box and setting it aside.
You'll come back to it later when your mind feels steadier.
This helps build confidence and trust in your ability to manage your emotions, even when they're intense.

Use simple, neutral thinking tasks to distract from emotional intensity.

Try naming fruits alphabetically, counting backwards by sevens, or solving an easy puzzle.
These activities occupy your brain just enough to interrupt the emotional spiral.
When your thoughts start to wander back to distress, gently return to the task, not to escape your emotions, but to give them space to soften.

Strong emotions can make you feel detached or numb. Sensory grounding helps you reconnect with your body.

Try eating something spicy or sour, holding an ice cube, smelling a strong scent, or running your hands under cool water.
These sensations anchor you to the present moment, reminding your nervous system that you're safe right now.

Reflection:

- Which ACCEPTS skills do you already use without realising it?
- Which ones feel most helpful when you're overwhelmed?
- Which feels uncomfortable or unnatural to try?

_____

_____

_____

_____

Distress Tolerance
Accepts Plan

Things I could do

How I could help

Things I have achieved

Things I could do

Things I could think about

Things I could do mindfully

Things I could experience

Distress Tolerance

The Self-Soothing Skill

Learning to self-soothe and self-regulate is essential.
As humans, we naturally seek comfort and safety through co-regulation, the calming presence of others. But co-regulation isn't always available, which is why it's just as important to learn how to comfort ourselves.
Self-soothing isn't about avoiding emotions; it's about creating a safe space within yourself while those emotions move through.
One of the most effective ways to do this is by using your senses.

Using the Senses

Your five senses can anchor you in the present moment and help you reconnect to your body. When you engage your senses, your brain receives clear signals of safety and calm.
A helpful way to prepare is by identifying what brings you comfort through sight, smell, taste, touch, and sound.

Collect these items into a **self-soothing sensory box**; a personal kit that supports you when emotions feel overwhelming.
It doesn't have to be a literal box. It could be a small basket beside your bed, a drawer, or a folder on your phone.
You might also want to create a smaller, portable version to take with you when you leave home.

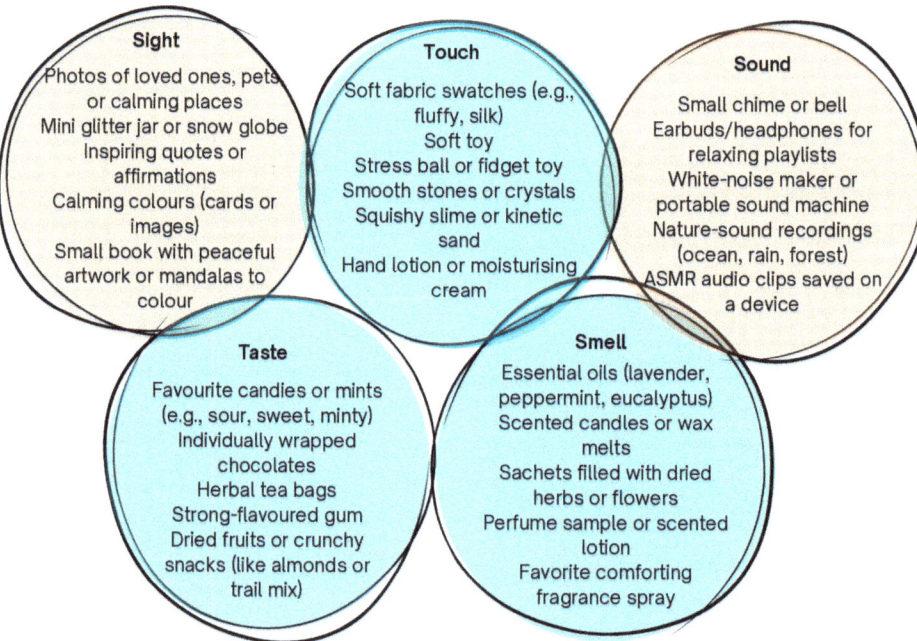

Sight
Photos of loved ones, pets or calming places
Mini glitter jar or snow globe
Inspiring quotes or affirmations
Calming colours (cards or images)
Small book with peaceful artwork or mandalas to colour

Touch
Soft fabric swatches (e.g., fluffy, silk)
Soft toy
Stress ball or fidget toy
Smooth stones or crystals
Squishy slime or kinetic sand
Hand lotion or moisturising cream

Sound
Small chime or bell
Earbuds/headphones for relaxing playlists
White-noise maker or portable sound machine
Nature-sound recordings (ocean, rain, forest)
ASMR audio clips saved on a device

Taste
Favourite candies or mints (e.g., sour, sweet, minty)
Individually wrapped chocolates
Herbal tea bags
Strong-flavoured gum
Dried fruits or crunchy snacks (like almonds or trail mix)

Smell
Essential oils (lavender, peppermint, eucalyptus)
Scented candles or wax melts
Sachets filled with dried herbs or flowers
Perfume sample or scented lotion
Favorite comforting fragrance spray

Distress Tolerance
Create your own

Things I like to see
_____
_____
_____
_____
_____

Things I like to touch
_____
_____
_____
_____
_____

Things I like to hear
_____
_____
_____
_____
_____

Things I like to smell
_____
_____
_____
_____
_____

Things I like to taste
_____
_____
_____
_____
_____

Things I can take with me
_____
_____
_____
_____
_____

Distress Tolerance

Radical Acceptance: Going Deeper

We've already introduced Radical Acceptance, but because it's such an essential part of distress tolerance, it deserves a closer look.

Radical Acceptance is about fully acknowledging reality, even when life doesn't unfold the way we hoped. It doesn't mean approving of what happened or forgiving those involved, that's a separate process. It means recognising that, despite how much we wish things were different, they are not.

Instead of staying stuck in bitterness; "I'm like this because of my past; life's unfair; why bother?", Radical Acceptance helps us shift to a mindset of "My past hurt me and shaped me in ways I can't change, but I can decide what to do next."

Resisting reality turns manageable pain into unnecessary suffering. Pain itself is inevitable, but suffering comes from fighting what is. When we stop arguing with reality, pain softens back into something we can manage.

Sadness or grief might surface at first, but those emotions eventually give way to calmness and relief. Many people resist acceptance because they fear this sadness, yet once they move through it, they often feel lighter and more at peace.

How to Practise Radical Acceptance

- **Identify the reality you're resisting.** Clearly name what you find difficult to accept.
- **Acknowledge your emotions about this reality.** "I'm angry." "I'm disappointed." Naming your emotions helps you face them.
- **Reflect on what changes when you stop fighting reality.** Notice how your body, thoughts, or actions shift when you let go of resistance.
- **Use accepting statements such as:** "I don't have to like this situation, but it is happening." "I can't control everything, but I can choose how I respond."

Radical Acceptance is not agreement. It's choosing peace over constant resistance.

Radical Acceptance is also recognising when you're not ready to accept something fully.

Even the simple act of noticing your resistance and acknowledging, "I can't accept this right now," is an act of Radical Acceptance itself.
You're still facing reality, the reality that, in this moment, you're not in the headspace to accept it. *That awareness is acceptance in practice.*

Distress Tolerance

Turning the Mind

Acceptance isn't something that happens once, it's a choice we make again and again.

Sometimes you'll find yourself turning your mind toward acceptance several times a day, especially when facing deep loss or disappointment.
Smaller frustrations, like no one wanting to watch your movie choice, might be easier to accept.
Bigger ones, like missing out on a dream job, dealing with illness, or grieving a loved one, require patience and repeated effort.

We call this ongoing process *Turning the Mind*, because Radical Acceptance is active. It requires you to consciously choose acceptance again and again, even when you slip out of it.

Imagine losing your keys. You check your pocket, they're not there. You accept it, then a few minutes later, you check again, hoping they'll appear. Radical Acceptance often works the same way. You might accept something for a moment, lose that acceptance, and then need to choose it again.

Radical Acceptance isn't about forcing yourself to be okay with what happened. It's about choosing to stop fighting the fact that you're not okay. You can accept that something is painful and that you're still struggling with it. Both can be true.

Acceptance Like a Wave

Imagine life as a series of waves in the ocean. These waves keep coming, one after another, whether you're ready or not. Fighting or resisting these waves won't stop them, instead, it makes you exhausted and overwhelmed. The best option is learning how to ride each wave as it comes, staying balanced, adapting to its movements, and becoming a better swimmer with every wave you encounter.

Reflection: Noticing Resistance

Before we shift from the mind to the body, take a moment to check in with yourself.
Where in your body do you feel resistance when you think about accepting something difficult?
Is it tightness in your chest, heaviness in your stomach, or tension in your jaw?
You don't have to change it, just notice it. *Awareness is the first step toward softening.*

Distress Tolerance

Using the Body to Accept

Sometimes, trying to change how we think or feel through logic alone can feel impossible. You can't always think your way out of pain or convince yourself to calm down, especially when your body is still holding tension.

In those moments, it can help to take a bottom-up approach, which means starting with the body and letting the mind follow.
Your body constantly sends signals to your brain about safety, threat, and emotion.
Think of your brain like a computer: the information it receives from your body (the input) determines the emotions you feel (the output).
When your body behaves in a way that matches calm or openness, your brain gradually aligns itself with that feeling.
This is because emotions aren't just thoughts, they're *physiological responses*, shaped by posture, breath, and movement.

Changing the body changes the message.

When you soften your shoulders, breathe slower, or relax your hands, you're telling your brain, *"It's okay. I'm safe enough to stop fighting."*
That's why small, intentional shifts in the body can create real emotional relief.
Two simple yet powerful ways to practise this are through **Half-Smiling** and **Willing Hands**.

Making a gentle smile can shift your emotions in subtle but powerful ways.

It might not make you happy instantly, but it can soften tension and open the door to acceptance.

1. Relax your face, neck, and shoulders.
2. Slightly lift the corners of your mouth into a half-smile, just enough to feel the difference.
3. You can even place a pen or pencil horizontally in your mouth to naturally lift the corners of your lips.

No one else needs to notice it. The half-smile is a quiet message of acceptance you send to yourself.

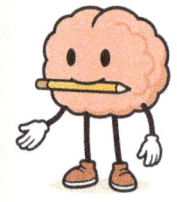

Your hands mirror your emotional state. When we're angry or resistant, our hands tend to clench or close.

Try instead the Willing Hands position:
rest your hands open with palms facing up, fingers relaxed, as if you're ready to receive something.
This simple posture communicates openness and willingness to your brain.
It helps release anger, tension, and the need for control.

Distress Tolerance

Reflection

Radical Acceptance is the bridge between awareness and peace. It doesn't erase pain. It removes resistance.
It's how we stop asking *"Why me?"* and start asking **"What now?"**

Every time you practice Radical Acceptance, with life, with others, with yourself, you're choosing freedom over frustration.
Acceptance is not surrender.

- What parts of your life or self feel hardest to accept?
- What emotions arise when you think about accepting them?
- How might choosing Radical Acceptance shift how you feel or respond?
- Try practising Half-Smiling and Willing Hands right now. What do you notice?

Shadow Work

Distress tolerance is the practice of staying with yourself when everything in you wants to run. These reflections invite you to notice what unfolds inside when pain, fear, or chaos arise. Pay attention to how your body responds, the stories that surface, and the parts of you that still search for safety in the idea that calm can only exist once the storm has passed.

- When things feel out of control, what part of me wants to take over; the fighter, the fixer, the avoider?

_____
_____
_____
_____

- What do I believe will happen if I don't "do" something immediately when I'm in distress?

_____
_____
_____
_____

- How did my family or early environment respond to pain or chaos? How might that still shape my reactions?

_____
_____
_____
_____

Shadow Work

- What helps me remember I can survive discomfort?

_____
_____
_____
_____

- What emotional triggers push me into impulsive behaviors?

_____
_____
_____
_____

- What reality am I currently struggling to accept? What emotions arise when I think about accepting this reality?

_____
_____
_____
_____

Emotional Regulation
made easy

Emotional Regulation

"Emotions are not good, bad, right, or wrong. The first step to changing our relationship to feelings is to be curious about them and the messages they send to us". - Marsha Linehan

What Even ARE Emotions?

Emotions are simply signals, messages sent from your brain to your body based on information gathered from your environment. They exist to guide you, not to control you.

Many people resist learning emotional regulation because they assume it means controlling their emotions. But emotional regulation isn't about control, it's about understanding.

The term "Emotional Regulation" is slightly misleading as, you're not learning to stop emotions from happening; you're learning how to manage your *behaviours in response* to your emotions.

Emotional regulation means acknowledging, naming, and feeling your emotions so that you can respond, **not react**.
It's what helps you create space between an event that triggers you and the way you respond to that event.

That space is where emotional intelligence lives.

> Mindfulness plus Emotional Regulation teaches us to put a space between an event that causes a heightened emotional response and our reaction to that emotional response.

Why Does It Feel Scary?

Our society has created strange rules around emotions. We hear about "good" and "bad" feelings, or "positive" and "negative" emotions.
Growing up, many of us were taught that showing emotion meant weakness.

Maybe you heard, "Stop crying or I'll give you something to cry about." or "Can you be a little less excited right now?"
No wonder so many of us became adults who either explode or shut down.
We've inherited generations of people without the language or tools to express their inner world, people carrying the shame of simply being human.

Your brain doesn't have a moral code when it comes to emotion. It doesn't know the difference between "good" and "bad." It simply registers emotion as information, movement, and sensation.
Each emotional experience floods the brain with a mix of hormones and neurotransmitters, a fun little chemical bath your brain really enjoys.

> ### What Emotional Regulation Isn't
>
> - It isn't about never feeling angry, sad, or frustrated.
> - It isn't about becoming emotionless or perfectly calm.
> - It isn't about being a "Zen master" who never gets upset.
>
> Emotional regulation is about recognising that not every emotion requires an immediate reaction.
> It's about giving yourself the chance to feel, understand, and choose your next step with awareness.

Emotional Regulation

Why Is Emotional Regulation Important?

When you can identify and express your emotions clearly, you gain more control over your life.
It brings clarity and connection, both to yourself and to others.

> Humans are simply a bunch of emotions in a trench coat, the quicker we become aware of the importance of understanding our emotions the easier our lives become.

What Does Emotional Regulation Do?

- **Reduces emotional suffering**: Understanding your emotions prevents unnecessary pain.
- **Prevents self-destructive behaviour**: Replaces harmful coping mechanisms with healthy ones.
- **Improves relationships**: Encourages communication instead of conflict.

Why It's Hard for Some People

Some people find emotional regulation especially challenging. Beyond biology and upbringing, our society doesn't make emotional regulation easy. We're encouraged to stay productive, stay positive, and keep going no matter what we feel. We praise emotional control but rarely emotional honesty.
Many people grow up believing that emotions make them weak, dramatic, or "too much." Others learn that it's safer to disconnect completely.

- **Biological Sensitivity:** Some people naturally feel emotions more intensely.
- **Lack of Skills:** You might never have learned how to manage emotions safely.
- **Reinforcing Behaviours:** Emotional outbursts can sometimes bring short-term relief (like attention or avoidance), which reinforces the habit.

Reflection: Emotional Learning

- How was emotional expression modelled in your family, culture, or community?
- What messages were you given about emotions, directly or indirectly?
- How might those beliefs still influence the way you express or avoid your feelings today?

_____

_____

_____

Emotional Regulation

Expanding Your Emotional Vocabulary

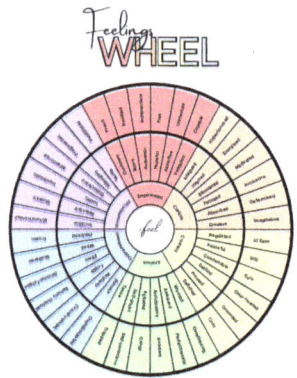

Our first step in building emotional regulation is increasing our vocabulary, giving our brain the ability to identify, name, or describe our emotions.

For many people, words like "sad" and "happy" are too broad in their ability to identify their emotion, but emotions are far more complex than that.

Naming emotions doesn't make them bigger, it makes them clearer.
When we give our feelings words, we take them out of the shadows and into awareness, where they become easier to work with.
It's the difference between being consumed by "something's wrong" and recognising, "I feel disappointed because I was hoping for something different."

Identifying emotions also helps others understand us. It builds empathy and creates space for meaningful connection instead of misunderstanding.
Your brain also loves clarity.
When you can name an emotion precisely, your nervous system relaxes because it knows what it's dealing with.

Identifying is a form of regulation.

What if I Can't Find the Words?

Sometimes emotions can feel like a language you were never taught.

Where you can sense something happening inside; a shift, a pressure, a pull, but you can't quite name it.
This experience is known as *alexithymia*, which literally means "no words for feelings."

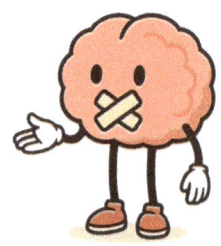

It doesn't mean you don't feel emotions; it means you experience them differently.

> **With alexithymia you might:**
> - Struggle to explain what you're feeling beyond "fine" or "off."
> - Notice your body reacts before your brain catches up.
> - Get frustrated when people ask "What's wrong?" because you genuinely don't know.
> - Confuse emotional sensations with physical ones; like a tight chest that feels like anger but could also be anxiety.

You might process feelings through movement, physical sensations, images, or creative outlets rather than through words.

Emotional Regulation

Finding Other Ways to Describe What You Feel

When you can't name the emotion directly, try describing what it feels like, rather than what it is.

You can start with body cues:

- "My chest feels tight."
- "I feel heavy and slow."
- "My stomach's in knots."

These can point toward emotions like fear, sadness, or anxiety.

Or describe your behavioural urges:

- "I want to disappear for a while."
- "I want to yell."
- "I can't sit still."

These clues can reveal what your emotions are trying to communicate, even if you don't have the right word for them yet.

The goal isn't to force language where there isn't any; it's to notice what your body is already saying.

Expressing Without Words

Not everyone speaks emotion through conversation.
Some people express it through sound, texture, rhythm, or colour.

Creative expression; like music, writing, or art can become an emotional translator.

Music:
Create a playlist for different moods. Sometimes the lyrics or melodies explain your emotions better than words ever could.

Art:
Paint, draw, sculpt, or even arrange objects in colour order. The process itself can clarify how you feel.

Expressive writing:
Use imagery instead of analysis. Try describing your emotion as a landscape, a season, or a weather pattern; "It feels like fog," "It's a storm that won't break," "It's sunlight that doesn't reach me."

These creative acts help you experience and release emotion rather than intellectualise it.

Emotional Regulation

Tools for Emotional Discovery: Feelings wheel

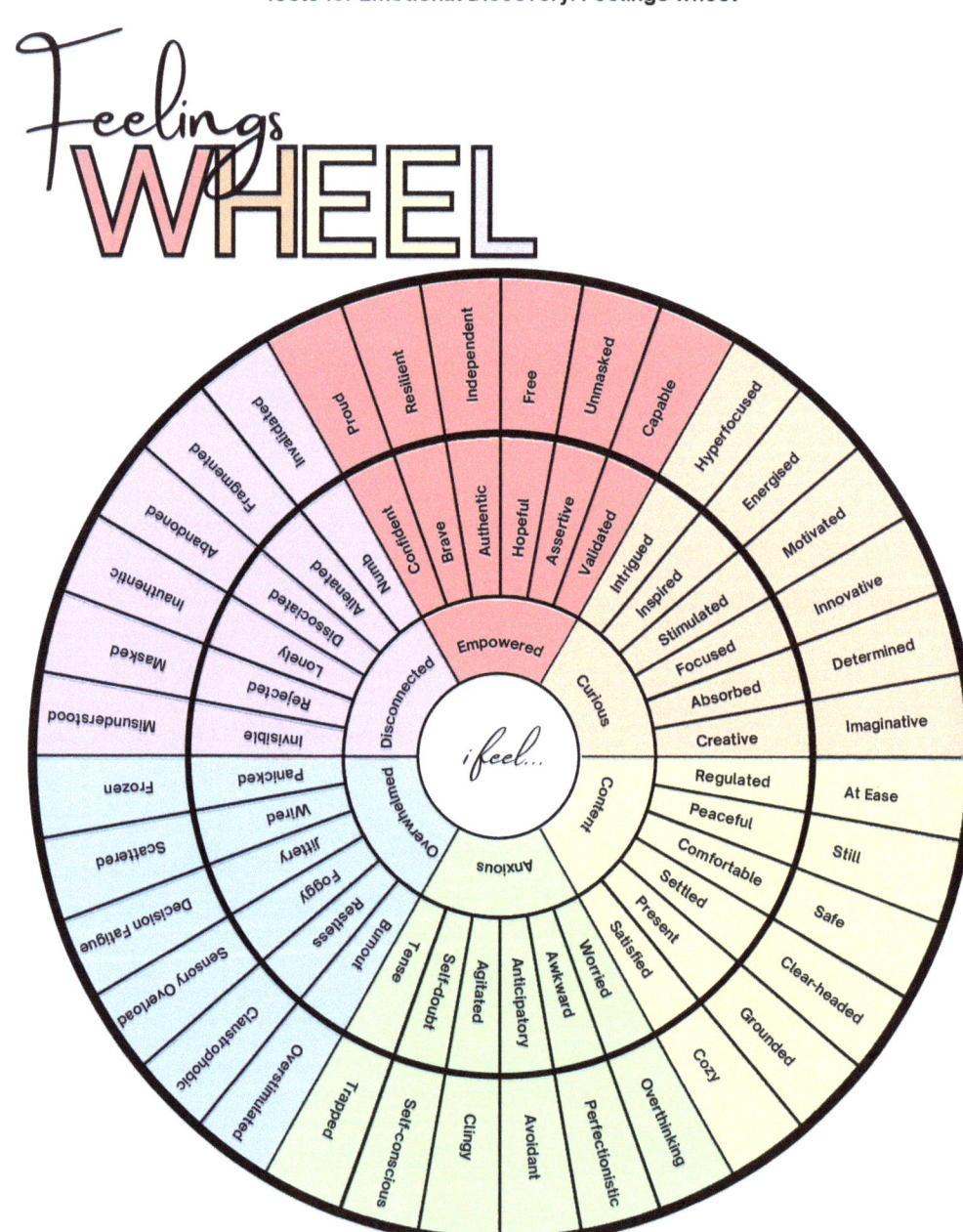

Emotional Regulation

The *Feelings Wheel* in this book is designed to help you recognise what's happening inside you; not by forcing labels, but by giving you language for your lived experience.

It's built around six emotional states that we move through regularly:
Empowered, Curious, Content, Anxious, Overwhelmed, and Disconnected.

Rather than dividing emotions into "positive" or "negative," this wheel focuses on how connected or regulated you feel. Each state expands into more specific experiences, helping you notice patterns, shifts, and needs.

For example:
- From Empowered, you might feel authentic, brave, or hopeful.
- From Curious, you might feel creative, inspired, or absorbed.
- From Content, you might feel peaceful, safe, or grounded.
- From Anxious, you might feel self-conscious, agitated, or avoidant.
- From Overwhelmed, you might feel frozen, scattered, or burned out.
- From Disconnected, you might feel lonely, rejected, or misunderstood.

You don't need to judge your emotions, they're simply signals showing how close or far you feel from yourself.

How to Use Your Feelings Wheel

- Pause and notice.
- When you feel "off" but can't name why, look at the wheel. Start at the centre and choose the word that most fits your current state.
- Move outward.
- Follow the ring outward to see if any of the more specific words describe your experience more accurately.
- Reflect on direction.
- Notice if your emotions are pulling you closer to connection and empowerment, or further into overwhelm and disconnection. There's no right or wrong place to be, just awareness.
- Use it for language building.
- The wheel can help you communicate emotions to others more clearly ("I'm feeling disconnected and misunderstood") or track patterns over time ("I often move between anxious and overwhelmed when I skip rest").
- Combine it with mindfulness.
- After finding your word, take a breath and check in with your body. Where do you feel this emotion? Is it tight, heavy, fluttery, numb, or warm?

Things to think about:

- Which section of the wheel do you find yourself in most often lately?
- What might your body be trying to tell you when you're in that space?
- Which direction on the wheel feels like "safety" or "home" for you?

Emotional Regulation

The Life Filter and the Stories We Tell

Every experience we have passes through a filter before it reaches our awareness, a lens built from everything we've lived through.

Our Life Filter is shaped by our upbringing, our relationships, our memories, and the meanings we've attached to them. It colours how we interpret the world, often without us realising it.

You and I could live through the same event and walk away with entirely different stories about what happened, not because one of us is wrong, but because we're seeing life through two very different lenses.

Imagine you message a friend, and they don't reply.
One person might think; "They must be busy."
Another might think; "They must be angry at me."
A third might think; "I knew people always leave."

Each of those thoughts tells a story, and each story says more about our filter than about the event itself.

We rarely react to life as it is. We react to what it means to us.

Seeing Through the Filter

Our brains are meaning-making machines. They connect dots, fill gaps, and build stories to make sense of what we experience.

This ability helps us survive, but it can also make us suffer.
When something in the present reminds us of old pain, our brain lights up with a familiar signal: *danger*.

That signal isn't always wrong, but it's not always right either. Sometimes we're not reacting to what's in front of us, but to something long behind us.

That's why we might spiral after a short text, feel abandoned after silence, or get angry at feedback that feels like criticism. The situation may be small, but the emotion is big because it's pulling on an old thread.

Recognising your filter isn't about blame; it's about compassion.
When you can see how your past shaped your reactions, you stop being at war with yourself for having them.

Emotional Regulation

Checking the Facts

Once you notice your filter at play, you can begin a quiet, powerful practice called Checking the Facts.
It's a mindfulness skill disguised as a thinking exercise, one that helps you separate what actually happened from what your brain added to the story.

When you feel a heightened emotional response after an event here's what you can try;

> Take a moment to ask yourself:
> - What did I observe?
> - What am I assuming?
> - What emotion am I feeling?
> - Does this emotion fit the facts?

Example:

You text someone. *They don't reply.*

Fact: They haven't responded yet.
Assumption: They're ignoring me.
Emotion: Rejected, anxious, hurt.
Re-evaluation: Could they be busy, asleep, distracted, or overwhelmed too?

What Happens When I Don't Check The Facts?

- Your loved one says they can't hang out with you today because they are not feeling well.
- Because of your life filter you believe they don't want to hang out with you because they hate you
- You cut them off, isolate, get angry at them, the relationship suffers or ends

You're not dismissing your feelings, you're just gently questioning the story that shaped them.
Sometimes, when we check the facts, nothing changes.
The situation still hurts. The emotion still feels true.
But we suffer less, because we're no longer arguing with reality; *we're simply acknowledging it.*

We are learning to approach situations with curiosity instead of expectation

Emotional Regulation

When Your Emotions Don't Match the Moment

Occasionally, checking the facts might reveal something else; that the emotion you're feeling doesn't quite fit the situation.
Maybe the reaction is too big, or too familiar, or belongs to a different story altogether.
That's when compassion matters most.

Your body remembered something before your mind did.
You don't need to push it away; you just need to bring *curiosity* to it.

Ask, "What is this reminding me of?" or "What need wasn't met back then that feels unmet now?"

Reflection

- Think of a recent moment where your reaction felt stronger than the situation.
- What story did your brain tell you about what happened?
- What are the plain facts, without interpretation?
- How does your understanding change when you separate the two?

_____

_____

_____

_____

_____

_____

_____

_____

_____

_____

_____

Emotional Regulation
Check the facts

Identify your emotion, what are you feeling? Write or draw

_____

_____

_____

Describe what happened using only logical facts Do not try to interoperate WHY

_____

_____

_____

Ask yourself, "What assumptions am I making? Are they definitely true?"

_____

_____

_____

Evaluate if your emotional intensity matches the reality of the situation.

_____

_____

_____

Emotional Regulation

Opposite Action: When Doing Changes Feeling

Once you begin to recognise what you feel and why it's there, a new question appears; *what now?*

Emotions are meant to move; they are messengers carrying impulses, stories, and memories through the body. They are simply signals from your brain about your current environment, and unfortunately because of our life filter, that information might not always be accurate. Every emotion carries a direction, and for the most part, those directions make sense. They keep us safe. They help us adapt.

But sometimes, the emotion doesn't match the moment.

The feeling might be real, but the situation may not call for what that feeling is urging you to do. You might want to disappear after a small disagreement. You might want to shout when someone asks a harmless question. You might want to run when all that's needed is a breath.

> Your emotions are always valid, but they are not always accurate. Your brain is interpreting your current environment using past information.

Opposite Action is about gently interrupting that automatic pull, not to silence the emotion, but to remind your body that there are other ways to respond.

> **Most of our reactions were learned a long time ago.**
>
> Maybe you grew up in a house where *conflict meant danger*, so now every raised voice feels like a **threat**.
> Maybe the people around you *praised strength but punished softness*, so you learned to **hide** every sign of sadness.
> Maybe you were taught that *being loved meant earning it*, so stillness feels **undeserved**.

These patterns don't make you broken, they make you human. Your brain isn't broken, it's working as designed to keep you safe. The information might just be a little outdated, and safety that was built for the past can start to feel like a cage in the present.

Opposite Action opens the door.

It invites you to do something small and different, just enough to show your brain that safety can look another way.
Each time you act differently, you plant a new memory, one that tells your nervous system;
"This moment is not that one."

Emotional Regulation

Practising Opposite Action

Opposite Action begins with noticing what your emotion is asking you to do, and then gently exploring what might happen if you did the opposite.
It isn't about forcing change or denying how you feel. It's about curiosity, and giving yourself permission to act in a way that supports your *future self* rather than your fear. Your brain learns new routes, new meanings, new ways of staying. Your brain creates new connections between situation and response.

Feeling	Learned response	Opposite action
Rejected: You feel unwanted or dismissed	Retreat, pull away, or shut down	Staying present; sending the message, finishing the conversation, or doing something kind for yourself that reminds you of your worth.
Inadequate: When you feel not good enough	Overwork, overperform, or numb out completely.	Rest; stopping, taking a breath, or doing something imperfect on purpose. You remind your brain that your value doesn't come from proving it.
Resentful: You might feel tight in your chest	Replay the story over and over, building the case in your head.	Shifting your focus; taking a walk, unclenching your jaw, or reminding yourself; "I don't have to carry this anymore." You create space for perspective to return.
Overwhelmed: When everything feels too much	Freeze, avoid, or shut the world out.	Doing one small task, asking for help, or naming what's actually in your control right now. Movement in any form helps the fog lift.
Hopeless: You feel like nothing will change	Stop trying altogether.	A single action; opening the blinds, making the bed, or walking to the mailbox. Tiny steps signal to your body that life is still moving, even if slowly.
Disconnected: When you feel detached or numb	Scrolling or isolating may feel easier than facing yourself.	Reconnecting through your senses; music, touch, light, taste, or movement. Grounding brings you home to your body, even before your mind is ready to follow.

Each opposite act is a quiet invitation; a reminder that emotion is movement, and that you have the power to guide where it flows.
The feeling might not shift right away, but your action still **plants a seed for change.**

Over time, your brain learns to follow your choices instead of your impulses.

Emotional Regulation

OPOSITE ➡ ACTION

When we move through life without awareness of our thoughts, feelings, or behaviours, our brain runs on autopilot. Over time, it starts linking certain feelings with automatic reactions, a behaviour it repeats without question. By bringing awareness to these patterns, we give ourselves the opportunity to pause, notice, and choose differently. Awareness is what allows us to step off autopilot and guide our responses with intention.

Emotion	Learned	Opposite

Emotional Regulation

How to Feel Your Feelings

Over time, our brains begin to associate certain emotions with pain. Maybe every time you cried, someone told you to stop. Maybe when you got excited, you were told to calm down. Or maybe when you were vulnerable, you were mocked or punished for it.

Slowly, your brain learned that certain emotions meant danger. It didn't matter that those emotions were completely natural, your brain isn't interested in fairness or logic when it comes to survival. It simply recognises patterns and creates rules to keep you safe.

If sadness once led to rejection, your brain learns that **sadness equals danger**. If excitement was met with embarrassment, then **joy becomes unsafe**. If vulnerability brought punishment, **being seen becomes threatening**.

As adults, we often find that these emotional "rules" still live inside us. When we feel sadness, joy, or vulnerability, the brain can react as though we're under attack. That's what happens when we're triggered: the amygdala (the part of the brain responsible for detecting threat) switches on, and suddenly we're no longer responding to the present, *but to the past*. Our heart races, our breath shortens, our body tenses, all to protect us from something that isn't happening anymore.

But emotions themselves are not dangerous.

They're not the enemy, they're messengers. Each one carries information about what we need or what matters to us. Learning begins when we stop trying to avoid, numb, or rationalise our emotions and instead start showing our brain that it's safe to feel them again.

Rebuilding Safety with Emotion

If you've spent time in self-help or therapy, you've likely heard to "just feel your emotions." For many of us, that never quite landed, especially if we're used to analysing feelings rather than experiencing them. The next exercise will slow this down and show you what it means to feel an emotion in your body.

Before you begin, gather a few tools: your feelings wheel, a sketchpad, or a journal where you can describe your emotional experience in words or images. Do a brief "*check the facts.*"

Choose a recent event that sparked a strong reaction or led to a coping behaviour you're not proud of. Separate what happened from what you felt happened. *That distinction matters.*

Now identify the emotion that was present. Use the feelings wheel to narrow it, sketch what it looks like, or write a few lines that capture its shape and weight. Once you have that emotion named or pictured, you're ready to move into the exercise.

Emotional Regulation

The Exercise

You'll need a quiet, safe space, somewhere your body can start to let go.

- Find a comfortable position. Let your shoulders drop.
- Look around your environment.
- Gently name what you see; "a chair," "a window," "light on the wall."

This helps your brain take in information that you are safe here, in this moment.

- Now, close your eyes.
- Bring to mind a recent situation or memory that stirred something big inside you; an argument, a disappointment, a moment of rejection.
- Try not to overthink. *Just notice what your body does as you recall it.*

Where does the feeling sit?

Is it a tightness in your stomach? A heaviness in your chest? A lump in your throat? Does your skin feel hot? Maybe it feels "icky" or "ugh" or "bleh". Whatever language or expression comes naturally to you. There's no wrong answer. *Emotions speak through the body, not through logic.*

- Place your hand gently on the area where you feel it most.
- Now we'll breathe, deliberately and slowly.
- Take a **double breath** in: Inhale through your nose once. Then, without exhaling, inhale again, a little more. (Like the stuttered breath before a cry.)
- Take a full breath out: exhale all the air from your lungs. Let your stomach contract as you push the last bit of air out.
- Say softly:

> "I feel ___." (Name your emotion, or describe it as best you can.)

- Repeat the double breath. Exhale fully. Then say:

> "I'm allowed to feel ___."

- On the third breath, inhale twice again, this time, tighten your muscles as you do it. Scrunch your shoulders, fists, face, everything.
- Then exhale all the air out as you release every bit of tension from your body.
- Say softly:

> "I am safe to feel ___."

- When you feel safe and ready, come back to your body and open your eyes.
- Notice how your body feels.
- Shake out your hands.
- Wrap your arms around yourself in a small hug.

Emotional Regulation

Why This Works

What this practice teaches your brain is **trust,** the kind of trust that says, "It's okay to feel this and still be safe."

This exercise helps you unlearn the association your brain might have between a certain emotion and actual real danger. By intentionally revisiting emotions in a safe, structured way, you show your brain that it can experience them without harm.

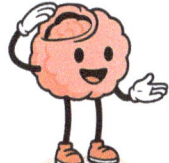

> The goal isn't to erase discomfort but to increase your capacity to stay present with it. Over time, your body learns that the feeling of sadness, anger, or fear isn't a threat, it's information.

When we manually slow our breathing and release physical tension, we stimulate the vagus nerve, which sends calming signals throughout the body. The double inhale followed by a full, controlled exhale is especially effective because it mirrors the body's natural rhythm during deep crying or relief. This tells your nervous system;

> **"You're not running. You're not fighting. You're safe enough to let go."**

Our emotions are physical experiences first. The shaking, crying, or heavy breathing we sometimes experience during distress are all built-in mechanisms for regulation. They're not signs of weakness; they're how the body completes a stress cycle. This exercise simply helps you access that same natural process consciously. So instead of reacting on autopilot, you begin responding with awareness.

The more consistently you practice this, the more your brain rewires its associations. You start building an internal map that says, *"I can feel deeply and still be okay."* This isn't about achieving calm; it's about learning that calm is possible even after chaos. Each time you practice, you're strengthening your emotional range, teaching your nervous system flexibility, and growing a sense of safety within yourself that doesn't depend on the outside world.

Reflection

What did you notice in your body before, during, and after?
Did the emotion change shape, intensity, or texture as you sat with it?

> **You don't need to analyse or fix anything, just observe.**

Maybe the feeling softened, maybe it stayed the same, or maybe new emotions surfaced. Whatever happens is simply information your body is offering you.

_____

_____

_____

Emotional Regulation

Building a Relationship With Self

The relationship you have with yourself shapes everything; how safe you feel in your body, how you connect with others, and how you move through the world.

Many of us grow up without that sense of safety.
Our bodies stay braced for what might go wrong, our minds replay every mistake, and our hearts wait for permission to rest.

Throughout this workbook we've touched on ways to build connection with self and to build safety in our bodies, but it is such an important topic that we should dig a bit deeper.

This part of the work is about rebuilding that safety, one small, human moment at a time. Not through control or perfection, but through the slow, steady act of showing up for yourself.

Start Small

A big reason we self-sabotage is that we try to *change too quickly*.
We leap toward huge goals, push ourselves into big promises, and hope momentum alone will carry us through. But when those promises are too big, they collapse under the weight of real life. You might tell yourself, "I'm going to the gym every day this week," and then only manage one day. You might declare, "I'm never eating junk food again," and find yourself in a drive-through after a stressful shift.

Every time this happens, your brain quietly takes note. It begins to associate your voice with unpredictability. Without meaning to, you teach your brain, "The things I say aren't dependable." Over time, this chips away at self-trust. It becomes harder to start anything meaningful because there's a deeper narrative running in the background: I don't follow through, so why try?

Not because you're lazy. Not because you're weak. Simply because your brain has learned from repeated evidence that your words and actions don't always match.
The way back is steadier and slower than most of us expect.
Self-trust isn't rebuilt through massive goals or dramatic declarations. It grows through small, consistent acts that reconnect the pathway between "I say I will" and "I did."

Try this:

Say the action out loud right before you do it.
"I'm going to pick up my water bottle," then pick it up.
"I'm going to take a shower," then walk to the bathroom.
These tiny steps teach your brain that your words have weight again. Each matched action becomes a small vote in favour of trust.

As you strengthen that connection, begin making slightly bigger promises:
"I'm going to answer that email today."
"I'm going to put the laundry in the machine."
Pair this with grounding techniques like slow exhalations or butterfly tapping; crossing your arms over your chest and gently tapping each shoulder in an alternating rhythm. This tells your nervous system, *"We're safe. We can do this."*

Emotional Regulation

Little by little, you create a new pattern:

When I speak, I follow through.
When I choose an action, I complete it.
When I show up for myself in small ways, I become someone I can rely on.

And from that foundation, bigger change becomes possible.

Getting to Know Yourself

There is often a wide stretch between hating ourselves and loving ourselves, and when someone says "just love yourself," it can feel completely out of reach. Expecting your mind to jump from one extreme to the other is unrealistic, especially if you've spent years relating to yourself through criticism or disappointment.

A gentler place to begin is neutrality; moving from self-hate to simple interest.
Not affection, not admiration, *just curiosity*.

Being interested in yourself is a far more accessible step. It lets you observe without attacking, listen without judging, and approach your inner world the way you might approach someone you're just getting to know. From there, the relationship has room to grow naturally, one small moment of attention at a time.

Who am I?

These questions help you notice the small, human things about yourself; the kind most of us never pause to explore. They build comfort before moving inward.

You can use these questions like conversation starters with yourself.
You might journal them, voice-note them, or answer them out loud on a walk.
There's no right way, the goal is to stay curious.

Warm-Up Reflections

- What are the small things that make you feel at ease in your day?
- What textures, sounds, or scents feel comforting to your body?
- What foods or drinks feel like a hug on a hard day?
- What colours or environments feel like a "yes" in your nervous system?
- When do you feel the most like yourself?
- What kinds of humour make you laugh without thinking?
- What activities absorb your attention in a peaceful way?
- Which parts of your daily routine feel like care rather than obligation?

Connection to Self

- What qualities do you appreciate in other people that you might also recognise in yourself?
- What compliments feel the easiest to receive, and why those?
- What moments in life have made you feel proud, even if no one else noticed?
- What brings out the softer parts of you?

These questions create the kind of familiarity you usually build when you're getting to know someone new; except this time, the relationship is with you.

You don't need to answer everything. Let the questions spark curiosity, not pressure.

Emotional Regulation

The Deeper Questions

Gently shifting from the outer world to the inner world.
These questions help you explore your values, fears, longings, and the parts of yourself that live beneath your everyday habits.

Understanding Your Inner World

- What experiences shaped the way you love, trust, or protect yourself?
- Which emotions feel easiest to express, and which ones feel more guarded?
- When do you feel the need to withdraw, and what usually sits underneath that?
- What makes you feel emotionally safe with another person?
- What kind of comfort do you wish others understood you needed?

Your Relationship With Yourself

- What do you admire in who you are becoming?
- What do you need more of from yourself?
- What do you avoid thinking about, and what might that avoidance be trying to protect?
- What would it look like to be on your own side more often?
- What parts of you feel overlooked or muted?
- What is one thing you wish someone had told you when you were younger?
- What dream or idea still gently tugs at you, even if you're unsure why?

Future Self

- How would your life feel if you trusted yourself a little more each day?
- What version of yourself are you slowly growing into?
- What steps feel kind and realistic for the person you are today?

Self-intimacy grows through questions, curiosity, and small moments of honesty.
These reflections are a beginning; an invitation to see yourself with the same interest you offer others.

Meeting the Layers within you

As you get to know yourself more deeply, you may notice that your inner world feels layered, with different tones, urges, or memories appearing as you reflect. We all carry many inner voices shaped by our experiences. Some learned to protect, some learned to perform, some learned to hide. Each one wants something for you, even if their methods can feel confusing or overwhelming. Each one carries its own history.

The more familiar you become with these layers, the easier it becomes to understand why you react the way you do, why certain emotions feel louder than others, and why change sometimes feels both comforting and frightening at the same time. IFS builds on this awareness by giving you a simple way to understand those internal movements and the stories behind them. It offers language for the parts of you that react, the parts that protect, and the parts that retreat. Moving into the next section, you'll learn how to meet these inner voices with curiosity so you can understand yourself with more clarity and warmth.

Emotional Regulation

Meeting Your Emotional Regulation Team

As you begin learning how to truly feel your emotions, you might start noticing that not every feeling comes from the same place. Sometimes you can sense *the part* of you that shuts down to keep the peace, or *the part* that jumps in to fix everything the second there's tension. There's another that gets angry when you're dismissed, and maybe one that just wants to disappear for a while.

It can be strange at first to realise there are so many different "yous" living inside one mind. But each part formed for a reason. Each one carries its own story about what it had to do to survive, to belong, or to protect you when things felt too overwhelming.

IFS meets DBT

To build a relationship with self we need to explore what The Internal Family Systems model (IFS) describes as our inner world or internal community; a collection of "parts" that each hold specific roles and beliefs. These parts develop naturally throughout our lives. When we go through stress, trauma, or even just repeated emotional experiences, some of these parts take on protective jobs.

You might have **a manager part**; the one that tries to prevent pain before it happens. It might plan ahead, overthink, perfect, or keep you endlessly busy to stay safe.	There might also be **a firefighter**, the part that reacts quickly when emotions feel too strong; distracting you with food, scrolling, work, or even anger so that you don't have to sit in pain.	And then there are **the exiles**; the younger, more vulnerable parts that carry the emotions and memories we pushed away long ago. They're the ones holding our sadness, shame, or fear, waiting for someone safe enough to listen.

None of these parts are bad or broken. They've simply learned how to protect you in the best way they could at the time.

The Self - The Calm Within

Beneath all of these inner voices is your **Self**; a calm, grounded awareness that isn't defined by any single emotion or part. It's the version of you that can listen with compassion rather than judgement, and curiosity rather than fear. When the Self is present, there's a sense of gentle leadership within; a quiet knowing that every part of you deserves to be seen and understood.
The more you connect with this space, the more your parts begin to relax. They learn they no longer need to shout or take over to be heard.

Emotional Regulation

Exercise: Getting to Know a Part

Take a few moments to think about a recent situation that left you feeling emotionally heightened. Maybe you said something you regret, shut down, or overexplained.

Bring that moment to mind and try to notice what part of you stepped forward. Was it the caretaker? The fixer? The avoider?

Try to get to know this part gently. You might ask yourself:

- What does this part believe it's protecting me from?
- How long has it been doing this job?
- What is it afraid would happen if it stopped?

You don't need to have perfect answers, even a vague sense of what it's trying to do for you is enough. Take a deep breath and acknowledge its effort.
You might say to yourself;

> *"I see that you're trying to help me. Thank you for working so hard."*

This simple recognition begins to build trust between you and the parts that have been running the show for years.

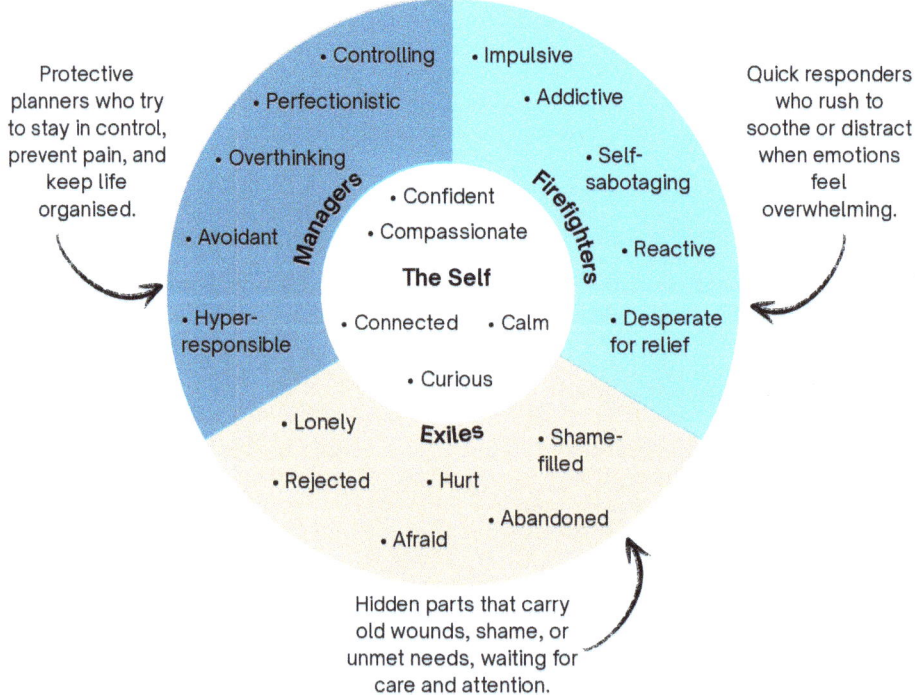

Emotional Regulation

Exercise: Creating Inner Space

Sometimes when a part is triggered, it can feel like it completely takes over; as though that emotion is you. In those moments, it helps to create a little distance between you and the feeling.

You can do this by shifting your language:

Instead of saying, "I'm angry,"
try: "A part of me feels angry."
Instead of, "I'm broken,"
try: "A part of me feels hurt."

It might sound small, but this change reminds your brain that you are more than any one emotion. You're the one who's noticing it; the calm observer, the Self.

Reflection

You might explore questions like:

- Which parts of me tend to show up when I feel unsafe or rejected?
- Which parts rarely get a voice?
- How do I usually treat my inner world; with curiosity, or with criticism?
- What does it feel like when I let my calm Self lead, instead of my protective parts?

Take your time reflecting. You might write, draw, or simply sit quietly with what comes up.

_____

_____

_____

_____

_____

_____

Emotional Regulation

What are the things that may prevent us from being regulated and in control?

Setting the Foundation for Emotional Regulation

There are so many reasons we might struggle to regulate our emotional responses. That's why this work has to begin with grace; understanding that regulation isn't about perfection, but preparation.
We can't expect ourselves to be calm, present, and grounded when our body or environment is constantly working against us.
To give ourselves the best chance at awareness and control, we have to care for the systems that keep us functioning; our body, our habits, our surroundings.

Physical health: How is my physical health?

> Pay attention to your physical needs. Address illnesses, tension, or pain rather than pushing through. The body you live in is also the body that feels for you.

Limit triggers: Is my environment full of triggers?

> You don't have to expose yourself to every stressful situation to prove strength. Identify what consistently overwhelms you and, when possible, create space from it. Regulation thrives in environments that feel safe.

Eat balanced meals: Has my body had any nutrients lately?

> Food is information for your brain. Eat consistently and in a way that nourishes you; low blood sugar alone can mimic anxiety or irritability.

Avoid mind-altering substances: Am I fully in control?

> Alcohol, caffeine, nicotine, and other drugs change your chemistry and make emotional balance harder to reach. Notice their effect on your mood, energy, and recovery.

Sleep health: Has my brain had time to recharge?

> A rested brain is a regulated brain. Sleep isn't a luxury, it's a part of your emotional hygiene. Keep a regular routine, even if the hours vary.

Exercise: Has my body moved today?

> Movement releases built-up energy and restores balance. You don't need an intense workout plan; a ten-minute walk, gentle stretches, or dancing in your living room all count. *Depression can't hit a moving target.*

Emotional Regulation

Weekly Check In

To support your emotional regulation, you can use the **PLEASE** skill as a simple weekly check-in.
It helps you stay mindful of the everyday habits that create a stable emotional baseline.
This isn't about perfection, it's about noticing patterns and gently adjusting where you can.

	Mon	Tue	Wed	Thurs	Fri	Sat	Sun
P							
L							
E							
A							
S							
E							

Reflection

- Were there any patterns you noticed?
- Add any notes you might have picked up on:

_____

_____

_____

_____

> Keep a weekly record to check in on creating the best environment to be emotionally regulated.

All behaviour is human behaviour.
And our mental health is inseparable from our physical health.

Emotional Regulation

Sleep; The Most Important Element

As we have now seen with the PLEASE skill, our mental and physical health are intertwined. When we are not looking after our physical health then it is much harder to emotionally regulate. However, out of all of the elements that make up our physical health, our sleep health is the most important.

You're not trying to sleep "correctly." You're getting to know your sleep patterns so you can work with them.

Sleep can often feel complicated. Many of us have nervous systems that stay switched on for longer, minds that jump between ideas, bodies that take time to settle, or routines that feel easier to maintain in some seasons than in others. We can approach these difficulties through curiosity, by helping you understand your sleep through patterns, habits, and small behavioural experiments. This is not meant to force your body into anything, instead we need to learn how to work with your brain's rhythms.

We will focus on rebuilding a healthy sleep system through four pillars: your sleep drive, your circadian rhythm, the way your mind relates to sleep, and the associations your brain forms with your bed and bedroom.

Understanding Your Sleep Pressure

Your body builds a natural pressure to sleep throughout the day. Some people feel this slowly, some feel it suddenly, and some feel it only after the world gets quiet. Sleep pressure can also often show up late or in unpredictable waves.

You can support this pressure by giving your body clear signals:
- waking up around the same time each day
- allowing yourself enough hours awake to feel naturally tired
- keeping naps short and earlier in the day
- spending the morning in light so your internal clock understands the rhythm

These small anchors create steadiness inside your system. Sleep becomes something your body moves toward, not something you have to chase.

Helping Your Brain Associate the Bed With Rest

Your bed often becomes a place of safety and decompression. It may hold scrolling, recovering from overwhelm, stimming, reading, or quiet withdrawal from sensory input. Because these experiences involve alertness, your brain can begin to link the bed with wakefulness.

You can help your system relearn a softer association. Moving toward bed when you notice natural sleepiness creates a clearer cue. If your mind becomes active or your body feels unsettled, stepping away for a brief moment allows the drowsy feeling to return. A wind-down area outside the blankets can also support this transition.

These practices create a gentle pathway between the end of the day and the beginning of rest.

Emotional Regulation

Navigating Busy Thoughts at Night

Night time often brings space for thoughts that didn't have room earlier. Memories, worries, ideas, problem-solving, and replayed conversations all tend to rise when the environment is calm. For certain minds, this openness can feel like a flood.

A simple way to support yourself is to give your thoughts a place to go. **Writing them down** helps them land. Acknowledging them without following them can create a sense of internal spaciousness. Touch, breath, or slow movement can offer your mind something steady to rest against.

These small rituals help the mind settle without needing to change or suppress its natural activity.

Understanding Your Internal Clock

Every nervous system carries its own timing. Some people feel most awake early. Others feel most alive at night. Many experience shifts depending on the season, emotional energy, or sensory load. Sometimes our internal clocks often move in patterns that don't match the external world, and those patterns still hold wisdom.

Supporting your clock involves gentle cues. Waking around the same time helps your system recognise the start of the day. Light in the morning and softer sensory signals in the evening help it understand the arc of time. When changes are needed, gradual adjustments tend to feel more approachable than abrupt shifts.
A steady rhythm forms when your body receives signals it understands and can rely on.

Caring for Your Sensory System

Sleep is a sensory experience. Light, texture, noise, temperature, pressure, and movement all shape the way your body feels at night. Sensory needs are wide-ranging, and the environment plays a meaningful role in supporting rest.

Your sensory world speaks directly to your nervous system, and your nervous system responds.

You might explore warm lighting, gentle sounds, a cooler or warmer room, softer or heavier bedding, familiar scents, or slow rhythmic movement. Some people settle with weight or compression. Others find deep comfort in very soft fabrics or a quiet hum in the background.

What This Work Creates

Building a relationship with your rest helps your body recognise safety and predictability. Over time you may notice that your system knows how to settle when it receives consistent cues.

Sleep begins to feel like something that grows through small daily practices, quiet support, and gentle self-understanding.

Your body carries its own wisdom around rest, and you're learning how to listen to it.

Emotional Regulation

Sleep Troubleshooting Guide

Use this whenever sleep feels confusing or unpredictable. Move through each step gently. There is no rush and no wrong place to start.

START
↓
Am I sleepy?

YES — Go to bed
↓
Are you in bed but awake for a while? (20+mins) → **YES** →

NO — Stay up and do something calming in low light
↓
Get out of bed
- Sit somewhere quiet
- Do something soft and repetitive
- Return to bed when feeling drowsy

Are your thoughts busy?
- Write down what your mind is holding
- Draw what your mind is holding
- Let the thought rest somewhere outside your body
- Using grounding to get back into your body

Is your body activated?
Adjust what you can:
- Temperature
- Noise
- Lighting
- Bedding
- Weight compression
- Movement or stillness

Find the combination that brings relaxation. Small adjustments create more settling than large overhauls

Do you easily wake up throughout the night?
- Caffeine intake and timing
- Heavy meals before bed
- Overstimulation before bed
- Inconsistent sleep/wake times
- Alcohol intake
- Stress/cortisol levels

Are you more awake after getting up?
- Stay out of bed until your body feels heavy again
- Avoid bright lights
- Choose activities that don't pull your mind too far forward

---

When sleep feels irregular over many days, return to the foundational cues: consistent morning light, a steady wake time, and small observations of what helps you settle. Patterns tend to reveal themselves quietly when you create space for noticing. Your nervous system holds a deep capacity for rest. These steps help you support the rhythms that are already within you.

Emotional Regulation

Different Ways of Thinking About Sleep

Many neurodivergent people carry a unique relationship with sleep. The way you feel about rest is shaped by your nervous system, your sensory world, your routines, and the expectations you've lived with. Understanding these internal experiences helps you move away from shame and toward curiosity.
Below are some common sleep experiences within neurodivergent communities, followed by reflections to help you explore your own patterns with warmth and care.

Revenge Bedtime Procrastination

Often the night can feel like the only time the world stops asking for things. When the day has been filled with decisions, masking, expectations, emotional labour, or sensory overwhelm, your brain may hold onto those late hours as a small slice of freedom.
This creates a pull toward staying awake longer, even when you feel tired. The quiet can feel sacred. There's finally time to be with yourself.

> **A gentle reframe:**
> Evening freedom can stay part of your rhythm. You're simply giving your body a structure that includes both rest and spaciousness. You can create a small ritual; a private moment, a quiet activity, a soft decompression window earlier in the evening, so your freedom doesn't always have to exist at midnight.

Nighttime as the Only Time to Unmask

When you spend the entire day navigating expectations, people, responsibilities, and social cues, your system may see the nighttime as the one place where masking drops away. This can make the night feel comforting and the idea of sleep feel premature, as if you're losing the only hours that belong entirely to you.

> **A gentle reframe:**
> You can create unmasked moments long before bed. A corner of your home. A sensory nook. A five-minute ritual. A consistent routine where you return to yourself. These moments allow your brain to exhale earlier, which helps rest arrive more naturally.

Sleep Feeling Like a Demand or Expectation

Sometimes we can feel resistance when something becomes a "should." Even something simple, like going to bed, can trigger executive dysfunction when it's framed as a task or responsibility. The idea of "you need to sleep now" can feel heavy, and heaviness often leads to avoidance.

> **A gentle reframe:**
> Instead of approaching sleep as a task, you can approach it as a transition. Transitions don't have to be perfect. They simply invite your body into the next phase of the day. A softer invitation eases the pressure: "I'm moving toward rest. I can take my time."

Emotional Regulation

Seeing Sleep as Losing Tomorrow Before It Starts

Some people experience a quiet grief when heading to bed, because sleep means the day is over and tomorrow begins. Tomorrow may carry expectations, decisions, responsibilities, or uncertainty. Going to bed can feel like stepping into the next set of demands before you're emotionally ready.

> **A gentle reframe:**
> Sleep becomes part of preparing for tomorrow with care. Rest doesn't force tomorrow closer; it gives your body more support to face it. You can think of sleep as an anchor between days, a pause, a reset, a moment where nothing is asked of you.

Feeling Like Sleep Is a Waste of Time

When your mind is full of ideas, tasks, obligations, emotions, or hyperfocus energy, sleep can feel like a disruption. The thought of lying still for hours may feel frustrating when there's so much you want or need to do.

> **A gentle reframe:**
> Rest gives your brain the fuel that makes those ideas and tasks easier to complete. Sleep isn't time taken away from your life; it's time that strengthens your capacity to live it. Your inspiration, creativity, and executive function often feel clearer when your body has had time to settle.

Creating a New Relationship With Rest

Neurodivergent sleep is deeply personal. You are allowed to approach rest in ways that honour your needs, your energy, your sensory world, and your emotional landscape. The goal isn't to change who you are; it's to create a sleeping environment and mindset that offers your nervous system space to breathe.

Some nights will feel easier and some nights won't. You're learning patterns, adjusting gently, and building a relationship with rest that feels sustainable. Over time, the way you think about sleep becomes softer, and your body begins to recognise that softness.

> Sleep becomes something you move toward with steadiness rather than something you have to fight your way into.

Emotional Regulation

Reflections

- When does the evening begin to feel like "my time"?
- What am I longing for during those hours?
- What parts of myself come forward at night that don't have space during the day?

_____

_____

- What truths about myself become clearer at night?
- Where in my day do I feel the most masked or compressed?
- What small pockets of unmasked time could I create earlier?

_____

_____

- What emotions come up when I think about going to bed?
- What does sleep represent to the part of me that feels resistant?
- What would make the transition into rest feel easier or gentler?

_____

_____

- What sleep patterns feel familiar from my past?
- What does rest mean to me emotionally, physically, and spiritually?
- What do I want my relationship with sleep to feel like in the future?
- What is one gentle shift I feel curious about exploring?

_____

_____

Emotional Regulation

The ABCs of Emotional Regulation

When we're learning new emotional skills, it's easy to focus only on fixing what's wrong, finding fault in our actions and surroundings, and constantly analysing and searching for answers. However, if you think of yourself as "self aware" yet you only ever focus on the parts of yourself that are "bad" or needing to change, then you are not self aware, you are simply being your own bully. When we only prioritise "removing the negatives", our lives will become dull and it will be easier to resort back to old, painful coping mechanisms. Regulation also involves actively finding and including positive experiences into our lives. That's where the **ABCs of Emotional Regulation** come in.

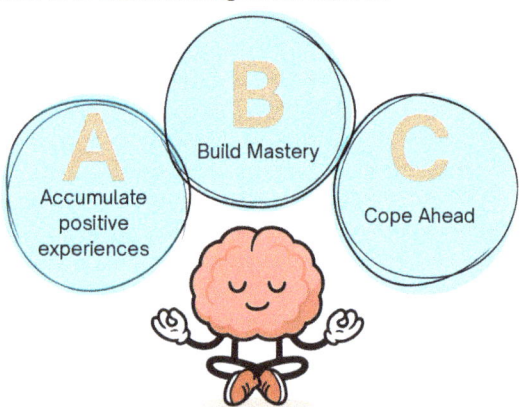

Accumulating Positive Experiences

This means actively seeking out moments of joy, curiosity, or calm. When mental health challenges make life feel small, our brains forget how to recognise pleasure or safety. You can't think your way into joy, you have to experience it.

Go outside. Try something new. Let yourself laugh, play, or explore without needing a reason. Each time you do, your brain learns that life can hold more than pain.

Building Mastery

Building mastery helps rebuild trust in yourself. It's about doing things that remind your brain, **"I can handle this."** It doesn't have to be impressive or public, it just has to be consistent.

Learn a recipe, fix something small, plant herbs, write a paragraph. Every small act of competence builds emotional stability.

Coping Ahead

Coping ahead is mental rehearsal; preparing your brain for difficult situations before they happen. Because your brain can't tell the difference between what's real and what's imagined, visualising success actually helps you perform better under stress.
Picture yourself entering the situation. See it clearly; the sounds, the words, your body language. Then imagine yourself managing it calmly and effectively. The more you practice, the more your nervous system believes, **"I've done this before."**

Emotional Regulation

Create your own action plan

Accumulate

What are things that bring you joy?

Build

What are some things you can improve?

Cope

Think of a future stressful situation, what fantastical outcome could possibly happen?

Emotional Regulation

Values: Your Inner Compass

When you understand what you stand for, your choices and reactions begin to make sense. Values act like an internal compass, when we drift too far from them, we often feel anxious, lost, or unfulfilled without knowing why.

If we say we value connection but constantly isolate, or if we say we value peace but fill our lives with chaos, that mismatch (known as cognitive dissonance) can create deep emotional stress.

Clarifying what truly matters to you brings alignment; between your inner world and the life you're living.

Why Understanding Your Values Matters

- **Clarity and Purpose**: Helps you make decisions that align with what's genuinely meaningful.
- **Emotional Regulation**: Acting according to your values reduces stress, guilt, and regret.
- **Life Satisfaction**: When your actions reflect your values, life feels fuller and more authentic.
- **Resilience**: Values give you a sense of direction when everything else feels uncertain.

Discovering Your Values

Reflection and Discovery

Think back to moments where you felt most alive, proud, or at peace. What made those moments meaningful? What values were you living by?

Prioritise

From the list provided, choose the values that feel most important to you right now. Not what you think you should value, but what your life is quietly asking for.

Align and Act

For each chosen value, set a goal that reflects it. Then take one small, practical step today.

For example:

- If your value is **connection**, your goal might be *reaching out* to someone you miss.
- If your value is **independence**, it might be doing one thing *alone* that usually feels uncomfortable.
- If your value is **peace**, it could mean decluttering a space or *setting a boundary*.

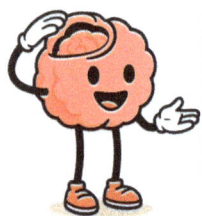

Discovering your values means identifying the principles and beliefs that matter most deeply to you. Your values guide your decisions, shape your goals, and influence how you interact with the world. Clarifying your values can help you create a life that feels meaningful, purposeful, and authentic.

Emotional Regulation

Living Your Values in Action

Once you've identified what matters most to you, the next step is finding ways to live those values in small, tangible ways that fit your current season of life. Living by your values doesn't mean changing everything overnight. It's about making daily choices that align with what you stand for. Below are some examples to help you begin.

Connection & Compassion
Values: Love, belonging, kindness, understanding, community.
How to live them:
- Call or message someone just to check in, without needing a reason.
- Listen to someone fully before offering advice.
- Volunteer your time or skills in your community.
- Set aside tech-free time for shared meals or conversations.
- Speak to yourself the way you'd speak to a friend who's struggling.

Integrity & Authenticity
Values: Honesty, responsibility, accountability, self-respect.
How to live them:
- Follow through on what you say, even when it's inconvenient.
- Admit mistakes openly and make amends when needed.
- Speak up for your boundaries instead of people-pleasing.
- Journal honestly about how you feel and what you need.
- Spend less time performing and more time being real.

Peace & Stability
Values: Calm, security, balance, grounding, safety.
How to live them:
- Create morning or evening routines that give you predictability.
- Say "no" to things that overstretch your energy.
- Practice gentle forms of mindfulness; slow breathing, body scans, quiet walks.
- Simplify your environment: declutter one space at a time.
- Seek relationships and spaces that feel safe, not chaotic.

Growth & Purpose
Values: Learning, progress, curiosity, contribution, meaning.
How to live them:
- Read or listen to something new every week.
- Sign up for a course, even just for fun.
- Reflect on how your past challenges shaped your current strengths.
- Do something that contributes to a cause larger than yourself.
- Keep a "growth journal" noting what you're learning about yourself.

Emotional Regulation

Creativity & Joy
Values: Expression, imagination, play, humour, inspiration.
How to live them:
- Engage in a creative hobby without judging the outcome.
- Dance, sing, or paint for the sake of feeling alive, not achieving mastery.
- Add beauty to your space; art, plants, colour, light.
- Curate a playlist that lifts your mood or sparks creativity.
- Notice moments of delight and document them (photos, notes, doodles).

Independence & Freedom
Values: Autonomy, confidence, self-reliance, adventure.
How to live them:
- Try doing one thing alone that you'd normally do with others.
- Make a small decision without seeking validation first.
- Spend a day exploring somewhere new, even locally.
- Build financial or emotional independence through small, consistent habits.
- Practise saying, "Let me think about that," before committing.

Achievement & Influence
Values: Success, leadership, progress, recognition, excellence.
How to live them:
- Set one realistic goal each month and track your progress.
- Celebrate achievements, no matter how small.
- Use your knowledge to mentor or support others.
- Share your work publicly instead of keeping it hidden.
- Create systems that help you feel capable and organised

Spirituality & Inner Guidance
Values: Faith, meaning, transcendence, intuition, connectedness.
How to live them:
- Spend time in nature or silence daily, even briefly.
- Engage in prayer, meditation, or personal ritual.
- Reflect on gratitude or what you believe in beyond yourself.
- Read teachings or philosophies that expand your perspective.
- Listen to your intuition; notice when your body says "yes" or "no."

Adventure & Curiosity
Values: Exploration, spontaneity, novelty, courage.
How to live them:
- Try something you've never done before; new food, route, or class.
- Say yes to a small risk that excites you.
- Take a "wrong turn day" where you intentionally explore without a plan.
- Talk to someone outside your usual social circle.

Emotional Regulation

Reflection

Take some time right now to consider the list of values on the previous page. In a perfect world, what would be important to you right now? Not what you think should be important, not what you think your parents or society might think is important. What is important to *you*.

Values

_____

_____

_____

_____

What are some goals you can set that will get you closer to living according to your values?

Goals

_____

_____

_____

_____

Goals without action are just words, what are some small, realisitic steps you can start implementing into your day to day?

Actions

_____

_____

_____

_____

Emotional Regulation

Building Your Identity Pillars

Now that you understand your values, it's time to look at the other pieces that make up who you are; the rest of your identity pillars.

Identity pillars are the aspects of your life that give it shape, structure, and meaning. They're the things that help you feel like you.
When our sense of identity rests on only one or two pillars, it becomes fragile. Small changes can suddenly feel like complete collapse.

> If your entire sense of self is built around your job, then losing that job doesn't just affect your income, it shakes your identity. If your only sense of purpose comes from being a parent, then when your children grow up, you may be left wondering who you are outside of that role.

The more identity pillars we have, the more stable our emotional foundation becomes. They give us balance, perspective, and a sense of continuity when life inevitably shifts.

Your identity pillars might include things like:

- Your relationships (family, friendships, community)
- Your work or education
- Your creative outlets or hobbies
- Your role as a caregiver, advocate, or learner
- Your connection to spirituality or nature
- Your physical wellbeing or personal growth

An identity pillar is something you invest in, not because you should, but because it brings you a sense of fulfilment or purpose. These are the things that make life feel full, meaningful, and worth showing up for.

If your current life feels unsteady, it might not mean something is "wrong" with you, it might simply mean that one pillar has been carrying too much weight for too long.

Reflection

Take a moment to reflect on what currently gives your life meaning.
- What roles, passions, or relationships feel central to who you are right now?

_____

_____

_____

Exploring and strengthening your other pillars can help bring your life back into balance.

Emotional Regulation

Mapping Your Identity Pillars

Use the picture below to fill out your own identity pillars

- In each column, write one role, value, or focus area that feels important to who you are.
- In the "core self" section write down your values, integrity or inner truth, the things that remain even if all your pillars fall (curious, resilient, focused, creative, ambitious etc).
- In the roof, either colour, draw or write what represents a "life worth living" to you, what life can look like when we have a strong foundation and a variety of pillars.

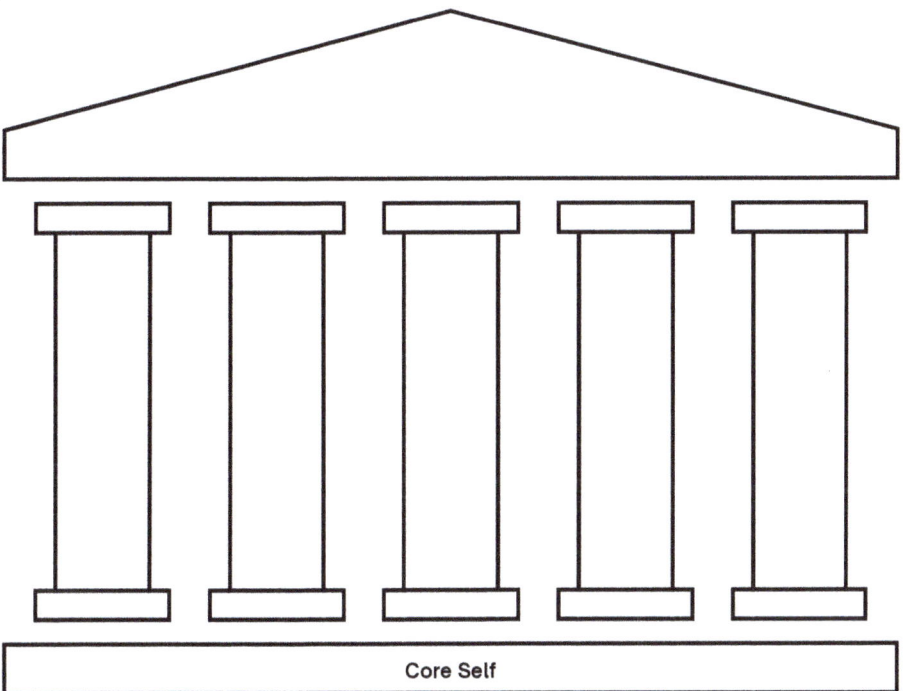

Reflection:

- Which of your pillars currently feels the strongest? Why?
- Is there a pillar that feels neglected or missing? What would strengthening it look like?
- Are there parts of yourself you've outgrown but still cling to?

_____

_____

_____

Emotional Regulation

Wrapping Up

Learning to regulate emotions is a process of *coming home to yourself.*

It's not a straight line or a perfect performance, it's a lifelong relationship with your inner world. This work is about noticing what's happening inside you, understanding your patterns, and gently guiding yourself back to safety.

Over time, that awareness begins to shift how you move through life.
Moments that once felt unbearable start to soften. You pause before reacting. You recognise that emotions don't have to dictate your actions, they can simply be information to understand and respond to.

And through all of this, it's important to remember: you are not broken.

Your brain is doing exactly what it was designed to do; *keeping you safe*. Every protective response, every reaction, every coping strategy once served a purpose. You're not undoing something "wrong"; you're simply learning new ways to live that fit who you are now.

Human beings are built to learn and adapt. That means there will be times when you return to old habits or feel like you've slipped backwards. But this isn't failure, it's just how learning looks in real life. You are working against years of automatic programming and survival patterns. Some days you'll choose the new skill, and some days you'll choose the familiar one. Both are part of growth.
What matters most is awareness, the moments you notice, pause, and offer yourself compassion. *That's progress.*

Every time you return to kindness instead of criticism, you're teaching your brain that safety exists within you too.

Take a breath and reflect:

- What have you learned about your emotions since beginning this chapter?
- What moments remind you that you can trust yourself again?
- How can you show yourself grace on the days when old habits resurface?

Emotional regulation isn't about becoming immune to emotion, it's about building trust that you can feel deeply and stay connected to yourself.
It's a practice of awareness, choice, and compassion, one that you'll keep refining, again and again, throughout your life.

Because being human isn't about being fixed. It's about continuing to learn how to meet yourself, over and over, with gentleness and understanding.

Shadow Work

This page is not about judging how "well" you've done. It's an invitation to pause, look inward, and notice what still lives beneath the surface.
Emotional regulation isn't just about learning new skills, it's about meeting the parts of yourself that once felt unsafe to feel.

Take your time with these prompts. There's no rush and no right answers. You're not trying to "solve" anything here, just to listen.

- When I think about strong emotions, what sensations or thoughts arise first? (Notice whether you feel tension, numbness, guilt, fear, or something else.)

_____

_____

_____

_____

- What emotions have I learned to label as "too much" or "not allowed"?
  (Where do you think those rules came from? Family, culture, or past experiences?)

_____

_____

_____

_____

- What does safety feel like in my body?
  (Describe textures, sounds, or memories that make your body relax.)

_____

_____

_____

_____

Shadow Work

- If I could reassure my younger self about emotions, what would I tell them? (Write as if you're speaking to a child who's still learning it's okay to feel.)

_____

_____

_____

_____

_____

- When I shut down or react impulsively, what part of me is trying to protect me?(Can you thank that part for trying to keep you safe, even if you no longer need its help?)

_____

_____

_____

_____

_____

- Are there emotions I avoid naming? Why?
  (Can you think of emotions that were labelled taboo in your upbringing?)

_____

_____

_____

_____

_____

Interpersonal Effectiveness
made easy

Interpersonal Effectiveness

Being skilled in *interpersonal effectiveness* means communicating your wants and needs clearly, while also respecting the needs and boundaries of others. It's the ability to express yourself in a way that doesn't activate the other person's defence system, in a way that doesn't feel like an attack.

This can feel difficult because most of us never learned healthy communication, we learned survival communication. Our tone, timing, and words are shaped by the homes, relationships, and environments we grew up in. If you learned to stay quiet to stay safe, your silence became protection. If you learned to fight to be heard, your intensity became survival. These habits made sense at the time, but they can create conflict in the present.

Healthy communication begins when we stop trying to "win" or avoid discomfort and instead start aiming for clarity, honesty, and connection.

Understanding Your Communication Style

Before you can communicate effectively, you need to understand how you currently express yourself. Everyone has a style that developed from their past experiences, and each comes with its own challenges.

People-Pleasing/Fawning

Putting others first to avoid conflict or rejection. Saying "yes" when you mean "no."
- Short-term effect: You feel safe.
- Long-term effect: You feel invisible, resentful, or misunderstood.

Avoidant/Withdrawing

Shutting down or disengaging instead of expressing what you feel.
- Short-term effect: You avoid discomfort.
- Long-term effect: Others experience distance or confusion.

Aggressive/Controlling

Expressing needs through intensity, volume, or criticism.
- Short-term effect: You feel powerful or "heard."
- Long-term effect: Others become defensive or withdraw.

Passive-Aggressive

Hinting, guilt-tripping, or using tone instead of clarity.
- Short-term effect: You release tension indirectly.
- Long-term effect: Misunderstandings and resentment build.

What is my usual way of communicating?
How does this style affect my relationships?

_____

_____

Interpersonal Effectiveness

Every Conversation Has a Purpose

Every time we communicate, there's a reason behind it; even if we're not conscious of it. We might be seeking validation, understanding, reassurance, connection, or attention. The problem arises when *the reason* we're communicating doesn't match *the way* we're communicating. If you're reaching out for comfort but speak with irritation, the person you love might not recognise the need underneath the tone. If you're seeking understanding but focus on defending your point, you may block the connection you were hoping for.
When you don't know what your own motivation is, the other person can't meet you there, because you haven't shown them where there is.

Clarity in motivation creates clarity in communication.

When We Aren't Clear

Alex grew up in a home where emotions were unpredictable. They learned to constantly anticipate others' feelings as a way to stay safe.
Jay, on the other hand, grew up in an environment where they were constantly criticised. They learned that being watched or questioned felt like being attacked.

In their relationship, these two patterns collide. Alex frequently asks Jay, "Are you okay?" to check the emotional temperature; a learned safety behaviour.
Jay experiences that same question as pressure and control, and reacts defensively. When Alex stops asking, Jay then feels ignored or unloved.

Neither of them is "wrong." They're both acting from learned patterns that once protected them. The solution starts with **understanding**: Alex's motivation is safety and connection, while Jay's is autonomy and freedom. Recognising this allows them to communicate what's underneath the reaction instead of acting from it.

When two people come together, so do their histories, their *life filter*. Each of us has learned different ways to protect, connect, and express. Those patterns can either complement or clash.
The moment we feel misunderstood or unsafe, our nervous system activates old strategies before we even realise it. Some of us pursue closeness to feel secure; others pull away to regain safety.

Both are valid. Both are human.

The goal isn't to erase these patterns but to recognise them as they happen. Awareness lets you pause before reacting, so the conversation becomes about the present moment rather than the past.

Interpersonal Effectiveness
Finding your motivation

What are you trying to get from the other person in this conversation?

___

What would be the perfect outcome to this conversation?

___

What am I unable to compromise on?

___

What happens in my body when I feel misunderstood or criticised?

___

Interpersonal Effectiveness

The Three C's of Connection

When it comes to relationships, people love to say communication is the most important thing. And while that's partly true, it's really only *one-third* of the picture.

Healthy, lasting relationships are built on what I like to call **the three C's**: Communication, Comprehension, and Compromise.

You can talk for hours and still get nowhere if the other person can't comprehend what you're trying to say. And even with perfect understanding, a relationship won't work without compromise.

All three need to work together for connection to last.

Every relationship is really just two (or more) unique worlds meeting each other; two nervous systems, two histories, two interpretations of what "safe" means. Each of us filters life through our life filter: the lens of our past experiences, beliefs, and memories.

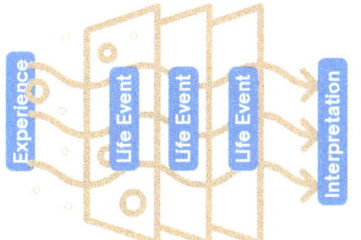

Our life filter shapes how we hear words, interpret tone, and decide what feels safe or threatening. Two people can live through the same moment and walk away with completely different understandings of what happened.

That's why self-awareness and curiosity matter so much.

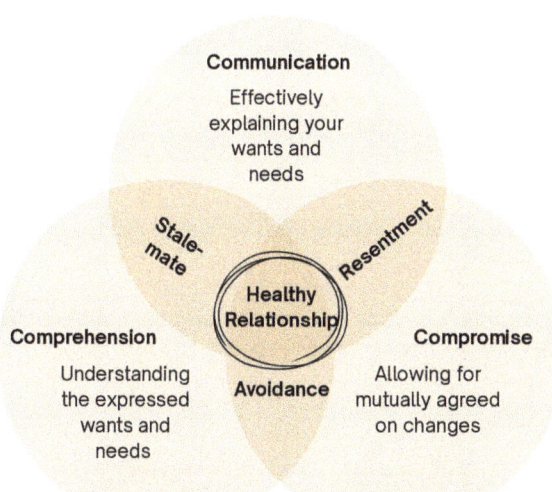

- Communication and comprehension without compromise can leave both people frustrated and unheard.

- Comprehension and compromise without communication can lead to silence and withdrawal.

- Communication and compromise without comprehension can breed resentment, because one person ends up feeling misunderstood while still giving up their needs to keep the peace.

Keeping all three in mind helps us stay open, humble, and connected, even when we disagree.

Interpersonal Effectiveness

Boundaries: Reclaiming Your Space

Relationships can be complicated, especially if you come from a trauma environment or if you're neurodivergent. You may have learned to mask or people-please from a young age as a way to survive. Maybe you were "the agreeable" child, or the "resilient" one who never needed anything.

That might have worked well for your family, especially if your caregivers were emotionally immature, but it isn't good for a developing brain. Learning early that you should push away your needs and focus on the comfort of others teaches your brain that you, the conscious person, don't matter as much. It tells you that other people's comfort is more important than your own.

Why is that a problem? Because humans are naturally self-focused. No one is born thinking their needs are unimportant. As a species, our babies are the perfect example of screaming, "Look at me, I'm important." Everything about us at birth, from how we look to the sounds we make, is designed to grab attention and care. We come into this world communicating; *"Help me, I matter."*

Unfortunately, through our environment and experiences, we can learn that being seen also means being punished. So our brains adapt. They learn how to keep us safe by helping us play small, agreeable, invisible. And we get rewarded for it.

"She's my easiest child; I never have to worry about her."
"They never ask for anything, not like my other child."

But ignoring your needs doesn't make them disappear. Just like the emotions we try to suppress, our needs grow and fester. They show up at inconvenient times, building resentment, pain, and self-abandonment.

This self-abandonment then creates the same behaviours that lead to abandonment, becoming a painful loop, a self fulfilling prophecy. The more we ignore our needs, the more our brains learn that we're not important, not worthy, maybe even *bad*.

So How Do We Change It?

We start by rebuilding our relationship with ourselves. We strengthen that relationship through awareness, consistency, and boundaries.

For many of us, the word "boundaries" carries discomfort.
That's usually because they were introduced too late, enforced reactively, or misunderstood altogether.
The truth is; *boundaries rarely feel good in the moment*, but they're essential for safety, respect, and connection. Healthy boundaries don't push people away; they make relationships clearer.

Interpersonal Effectiveness

Boundaries vs. Expectations vs. Rules

People often confuse these three, so let's separate them clearly.

Boundaries: What I Will Do to Protect My Well-Being

A boundary is about you, not the other person. It's a statement of what you will or will not allow in your emotional or physical space.

> "If you raise your voice at me, I will end the conversation and walk away."
>
> Boundaries are self-directed. They are not punishments or attempts to make someone change.
> They are acts of self-respect, ways to protect your energy, peace, and dignity.
>
> You can think of them as:
> - "If you do ___, I will ___."
> - "I won't ___."
> - "If this happens, I will ___."

Boundaries remind you that you can't control others, but you can control your own choices and responses.

Setting them often feels wrong at first, especially if you've spent your life avoiding conflict or keeping the peace. When you start setting boundaries, some people may not react well. If they're used to you being compliant, your "no" might sound like rejection. This is normal. It means you're breaking an old pattern, not doing something wrong.

You're teaching your brain that safety includes you too.

Expectations: What I Hope or Want Others to Do

An expectation is about someone else's behaviour; what you hope they will do.

> "I expect my partner to be loyal to me."
>
> There's nothing wrong with having expectations; they're part of all healthy relationships. The issue arises when we treat them as boundaries.
> A boundary isn't what you hope someone will do, it's what you'll do *if your expectation isn't met.*
>
> "If my partner cheats, I will end the relationship."

Expectations are *hopes*; boundaries are **actions**. Knowing the difference shifts your focus from what others should do to what you can control.

Interpersonal Effectiveness

Rules: Attempts to Control Others

A rule is something you try to impose on another person. It tells them what they must or must not do.

> "You're not allowed to talk to your ex."
>
> Rules come from fear and control, not respect or trust. They can create resentment, power struggles, and, ironically, the disconnection we were trying to avoid.
>
> This is especially common for people who fear abandonment. Rules may feel protective, but the safety they create is temporary and fragile.
>
> Healthy relationships are built on **boundaries**, not rules. Boundaries give each person the freedom to choose, and the responsibility to face the consequences of their choices.

If you feel tempted to set a rule, try reframing it into a boundary:

- Instead of: "You're not allowed to talk to your ex,"
- Try: "If you choose to stay in contact with your ex, I'll need to consider whether this relationship still feels safe for me."

This version keeps both autonomy and accountability intact.

Why Boundaries Matter

Boundaries are the meeting point between your needs and your values.
They preserve your sense of self while still allowing connection.

When done well, they:

- Build mutual trust and emotional safety
- Reduce resentment and burnout
- Encourage honesty and accountability
- Strengthen self-respect and emotional stability

But perhaps most importantly; they remind you that *your needs are valid*, and **your** comfort matters too.

> When you start setting boundaries, not everyone will welcome the change. If people are used to you being easy-going or accommodating, your new limits might feel uncomfortable or even like rejection. This is especially true in families with low emotional maturity or in cultures where questioning elders is seen as disrespectful.

Interpersonal Effectiveness

Bridging Into Communication

Now that you've explored what your boundaries are and why they matter, the next step is learning how to communicate them in a way that honours both you and the relationship. It's one thing to know where your limits are; it's another to express them calmly, clearly, and without losing connection.

This is where many of us get stuck. We might know we're uncomfortable or hurt, but struggle to find the words, or fear the reaction we'll get if we speak up. Some of us were taught that asserting ourselves was selfish or rude, while others learned that conflict meant danger.

Healthy communication isn't about being agreeable or never upsetting anyone. It's about expressing your truth in a way that is respectful, direct, and grounded. That's exactly what the DEARMAN skill helps you do.
It provides a simple framework for expressing what you need, asking for change, or saying no, while maintaining self-respect and protecting the relationship.

This inability to express ourselves can often lead to damaging behaviours like "testing" people, staying quiet or dropping hints, then becoming resentful when our needs aren't met.

Before we begin, take a moment to remember that communication is a skill, not a personality trait. It's something we can learn, practice, and strengthen over time.
You don't have to get it perfect. You just have to stay curious, compassionate, and willing to keep trying.

Communication Is a Two Way Street

It also helps to remember that other people have their own communication histories too. Their defensiveness, avoidance, or intensity often come from the same place yours does; fear, shame, or a need to feel safe. Understanding this doesn't excuse poor behaviour, but it does help you navigate conversations with more empathy and less reactivity.
The DEARMAN skill is one of the most practical ways to bridge this gap, between emotion and expression, between intention and impact. It provides structure so that your needs and feelings can be expressed clearly, without losing connection or self-respect.

Reflection Prompt: Communication Awareness

Take a few moments to think about the communication style you learned growing up.
- How did your caregivers express anger, sadness, or affection?
- What messages did you receive about speaking up for yourself?
- How do those patterns still show up in your relationships today?

_____

_____

_____

Interpersonal Effectiveness

Once you've taken the time to understand your motivation for a conversation; what you really want or need, the DBT skill DEARMAN helps you express that in a clear, calm, and effective way.
It's especially useful when emotions are high or when you're worried about how the other person might react. Think of it as a structure that helps you stay grounded and assertive while still being kind.

D.E.A.R.M.A.N *skill*

Describe the situation. Just state the facts, not your feelings or thoughts about it. This helps regulate the conversation. Facts feel safe, predictable, and less overwhelming.

- Use clear, direct language. Avoid over-detailing or tangents (common when you're anxious or hyperfocused).
- Try writing your thoughts down first if verbal expression feels hard.
- Stick to observable facts: who, what, when, where.

Example:
"When you cancelled our plans last minute, I felt disappointed because I was looking forward to it."

Express how you feel or what you need using "I" statements.
This step can feel uncomfortable, especially if you're used to hiding or minimising your emotions to avoid rejection.

You might have difficulty identifying emotions, so it can help to name physical sensations instead of emotional labels: "My chest felt tight," or "I started to shut down."
- You don't need to perform emotion. A calm, monotone expression can still carry meaning.
- Remember that expressing feelings is not dramatic, it's clarifying.

Example:
"I felt anxious and a bit hurt when you didn't reply."

Assert what you want or need clearly, or say NO clearly.

- Script it beforehand if that helps you feel grounded.
- Be literal and concise; avoid hinting or hoping they'll "get it."
- It's okay to use alternate formats, like texting or emailing, if in-person feels too intense.

Example:
"I need you to let me know if you can't make it next time, instead of cancelling last minute."
You're not demanding, you're being clear.

Reinforce means explaining why your request makes sense or benefits the relationship. This isn't manipulation; it's helping the other person understand your logic.

- Logic can be grounding. Explaining "why" in a structured way can reduce misinterpretation.
- But don't over-reinforce, you don't have to over-justify your needs.

Example:
"If you tell me earlier, it helps me manage my time and not spiral into anxiety."

Interpersonal Effectiveness

Mindful, this step is about staying focused on your goal.
It's easy to get derailed when conversations become emotional or confusing.

- You may hyperfocus on fairness, side topics, or tone policing, notice when that happens and gently bring yourself back.
- You can use notes or written reminders during the conversation to stay on track.
- If you get overwhelmed, it's okay to ask for a break: "I want to keep talking, but I need a moment to regulate."

Anchor yourself in calm and confidence. This doesn't mean pretending to be calm, it means grounding your body so your words come from stability, not panic.

- You might not "look confident," but you can feel anchored.
- Focus on steady breathing, gentle stimming, or keeping one phrase in mind that centres you, like "I'm safe to speak."
- Let your body find its own version of calm; rocking, holding something tactile, pacing slowly, or sitting still.

Example:
"I know what I'm asking for is fair, even if it feels uncomfortable."
Anchoring keeps your message clear even when your emotions or sensory environment feel intense.

Negotiation means finding balance. Be flexible while maintaining self-respect.

- It's okay to ask for time before deciding: "I need to think about that."
- You can offer alternatives that meet both people's needs.
- Remember that compromise doesn't mean self-abandonment.
- Example:
- "If you can't commit right away, can you let me know by tomorrow instead?"
- Negotiation is about collaboration, not compliance.

A Note on Communication and Neurodivergent Communication

Learning to communicate effectively isn't about masking who you are or forcing yourself to sound "acceptable."
It's about understanding how you communicate, and learning the tools to make that communication clearer, safer, and more effective for you and others.

Many neurodivergent people have communication styles that differ from neurotypical expectations. You might communicate directly, use less eye contact, rely on written messages, or need more time to process before responding. **None of that is wrong.**
These skills aren't about becoming more agreeable or palatable; they're about *recognising patterns*; both yours and those of others, so that conversations become easier to navigate and less likely to spiral into misunderstanding or manipulation.
Being aware of your communication style doesn't make you less authentic; *it gives you choice.*
You learn when to explain your differences, when to take space, and how to express your needs in a way that honours both you and the person you're speaking to.
It's not about talking differently, it's about being understood and not taken advantage of.

Interpersonal Effectiveness

Reflection: Understanding My Communication Style

Developing awareness means you can stay authentically you while still communicating clearly enough to be understood.
You can hold your truth without shrinking it down to fit someone else's comfort.
You can also begin to see the communication patterns of others; their tone, pace, and reactions as information, not intimidation.
When you can notice rather than internalise those patterns, *you're already communicating more effectively than most.*

Take a moment to explore how your communication works.
These reflections can help you recognise your strengths, your triggers, and the places where misunderstanding tends to happen.

Journal Prompts

- How do I usually express myself when I'm calm? How does that change when I'm stressed or overstimulated?

_____

_____

- What forms of communication (text, voice, writing, gestures) feel most natural to me? Which ones drain me?

_____

_____

- When do I feel most misunderstood, and what's usually happening in those moments?

_____

_____

- When do I feel pressured to mask or perform in conversation? What does that cost me emotionally?

_____

_____

- What kinds of communication from others make me feel safe or unsafe?

_____

_____

Interpersonal Effectiveness
Plan your own DEARMAN conversation

D — Describe

E — Express

A — Assert

R — Reinforce

M — Mindful

A — Anchor

N — Negotiate

Interpersonal Effectiveness

Protecting The Relationship

Boundaries are an essential part of building a healthy relationship with yourself. They remind you that your needs matter, that your voice deserves space, and that you are responsible for your own well-being.
At the same time, *relationships are living things;* they breathe, shift, and adapt. Learning to honour your boundaries also means learning how to stay connected while doing so. That balance takes practice, compassion, and awareness.

As we begin to protect our sense of self, it's easy to fall into all-or-nothing thinking. Some people hold their boundaries so tightly that they push others away, while others bend so often that they lose sight of themselves. The goal isn't to choose between self-protection and connection, but to create a steady relationship between the two, one that can hold both honesty and care.

GIVE

One of the ways we can learn this balance is **GIVE**; a skill designed to soften defensiveness and foster emotional safety in conversations.

When you use **GIVE**, you're not focusing on winning or being perfect. You're focusing on connection, on staying present long enough for real communication to happen.

When we approach a conversation with the goal of proving a point or being right, the other person often senses that energy before we even say a word. Our tone, body language, and facial expressions can all signal threat. Human brains are wired to detect emotional cues, often faster than logic can catch up. Once the nervous system detects danger, communication shifts into survival mode. The amygdala activates, and the part of the brain responsible for understanding and problem-solving temporarily goes offline.

From there, things escalate quickly. Even calm discussions can turn defensive, as both people instinctively try to protect themselves. The words may still sound polite, but the energy underneath feels sharp. *Everyone is listening to react, not to understand.*

The purpose of GIVE is to change that pattern.
It helps you slow down the emotional pace of a conversation so that safety can return, both for you and the other person. It's not about being passive or pretending everything is fine; it's about communicating in a way that keeps both people's nervous systems in a state of balance, where genuine understanding becomes possible.

> *The most powerful conversations don't come from control. They come from safety and vulnerability*

Interpersonal Effectiveness

These skills take practice, especially if you've spent years learning that communication equals conflict. But GIVE reminds us that communication isn't just about speaking; it's about creating an emotional space where both people can show up as human, without needing to win or withdraw.

Be GENTLE

Being gentle is about your approach, not about being submissive.
It means speaking in a way that reduces defensiveness, both in yourself and the other person.
This might mean regulating your nervous system first before engaging. You cannot sound or feel gentle when your body is in fight, flight, or shutdown.

Being gentle might look like:
- Taking a sensory break before a hard conversation.
- Using written communication if speaking face-to-face feels too activating.
- Choosing words that are straightforward instead of emotional or dramatic.
- Speaking softly but firmly: "I want to talk about this, but I need us both to stay calm."
- Being gentle is not about suppressing emotion; it's about communicating from your regulated self instead of your reactive self.

Be INTERESTED

Being interested means showing that you are present and engaged.
This can be difficult for people who may mask interest differently, or our natural body language doesn't align with societal expectations.
You do not need to force eye contact or mirror someone's tone to show interest. Instead, focus on curiosity. Genuine curiosity about what the other person is saying or feeling.

Being interested might look like:
- Saying, "I'm listening, I just need to look away while I process."
- Nodding or summarising what you heard: "So you felt ignored when that happened?"
- Asking clarifying questions instead of assuming.
- Interest is about connection, not performance. You can be quiet, fidgety, or avoidant of eye contact and still be deeply interested.

Be VALIDATING

You might struggle to validate others when their emotions feel unpredictable or unsafe, especially if you've spent years invalidating yourself.
Validation does not mean you have to agree or surrender your perspective. It means saying, "I see that this is real for you."

Being validating can sound like;
- "I can see why that would upset you."
- "That makes sense, given what you've been through."
- "I get that this feels unfair, even if I see it differently."

Validation can also mean self-validation. Before or after the conversation, remind yourself:
"My feelings make sense too. My brain is just wired to notice different things."
Validation helps lower shame and opens the door for real problem-solving.

Interpersonal Effectiveness

To be engaged means approaching the conversation with calmness and openness. It is about bringing steady energy into your interactions instead of tension or defensiveness.

This can mean paying attention to your tone, pace, and body language in ways that feel authentic and sustainable for you. You do not need to force eye contact, smile constantly, or pretend to be relaxed. Instead, focus on creating a sense of safety, both for yourself and the other person.

Being engaged can look like:
- Taking a deep breath before speaking.
- Keeping your tone steady and your words clear.
- Using gentle humour or warmth if it feels natural.

To be engaged means to communicate from a grounded place. It helps others feel safe enough to listen, and it helps you stay connected to your message without shutting down or attacking.

Reflection: Practising Connection Through GIVE

Every conversation carries an energy.
Sometimes we enter with *curiosity*, other times with tension or fear.
Before reacting, pause and ask yourself:

- What energy am I bringing into this conversation?
- What might the other person's nervous system be picking up from me right now?
- How can I create safety for both of us while still honouring my truth?

Try to think of a recent interaction, maybe one that left you feeling unheard, misunderstood, or defensive.

If you could replay that moment using the GIVE skill, what might have changed?
Would being gentler, more curious, validating, or engaged have helped you stay connected?

Take a few notes below about what you notice.

_____

_____

_____

_____

Interpersonal Effectiveness

After learning how to communicate in ways that build safety and understanding with others, the next step is learning how to protect that same safety within yourself. Relationships thrive on connection, but connection isn't sustainable if it costs your integrity. This is where the next skill, **FAST**, comes in; a way to stay honest, grounded, and respectful without losing your sense of self in the process.

To be fair means to respect both yourself and the other person. It's not about being neutral or giving everyone the same amount of space. It's about balance.
Being fair often starts with remembering that your perspective matters too. You may have learned to over-accommodate others to avoid conflict, which can make fairness feel selfish. But it isn't selfish, it's equal.

Being fair might look like:
- Saying, "I understand how you feel, and this is how I see it."
- Avoiding the instinct to over-explain to prove you're good or right.
- Checking in with yourself: "Am I giving empathy to others but denying it to myself?"

Being fair means seeing the humanity in both people, including you.

To be accountable means taking responsibility for your actions and their impact, without slipping into guilt or over-apology.
It's the balance between acknowledging your part and remembering that not everything is yours to carry.
This can mean unlearning the habit of apologising for existing, for feeling too much, or for communicating differently.

Accountability is about truth, not shame.
It might sound like:
- "I see how what I said hurt you, that wasn't my intention."
- "I misunderstood that, but I'd like to clarify."
- "I can take responsibility for my tone, but not for your interpretation."

To be accountable is to show integrity, owning what's yours while refusing to own what isn't.

To be steadfast means standing firm in your values and boundaries, even when it's uncomfortable. It's about trusting your internal compass when external pressure tells you to bend.
This can be especially hard. Many of us learned to mask or people-please to survive, which often meant betraying our values for belonging. Being steadfast is how you begin to rebuild that lost self-trust.

It might sound like:
- "I value honesty, so I'm going to be clear, even if it's awkward."
- "I won't continue this conversation if I'm being yelled at."
- "I know what's right for me, and I'm not going to apologise for that."

Steadfastness is not rigidity. It's holding your values with calm strength, knowing they can guide you even when emotions run high.

Interpersonal Effectiveness

To be truthful means being authentic, direct, and consistent. It's not about harsh honesty or saying everything you think. It's about aligning your words with your truth instead of hiding behind what feels safer.

This can be complicated. Many of us have been punished for being "too honest" or for expressing truth bluntly. To be truthful here means to speak from authenticity and emotional awareness.

It might sound like:
- "That comment hurt my feelings."
- "I don't agree, but I respect your perspective."
- "I need time to process before I respond."

Truthfulness builds safety and trust, both with others and within yourself.

Reflection: Holding Integrity in Conversation

When you speak your truth;
- How does your body respond?
- Do you notice tension, guilt, or relief?
- Where do you feel it most; your chest, your throat, your stomach?

Take a moment to think about a recent interaction where you walked away feeling uneasy or proud of how you handled yourself.

Ask yourself:
- Was I being fair to myself and the other person?
- Did I take accountability where it was mine to take? And let go of what wasn't?
- Did I stay true to my values, even if it felt uncomfortable?
- Did I speak honestly, or did I hide behind what felt safer?

Write down what you notice. There's no need to judge your answers; this is about awareness, not perfection.

_____

_____

_____

_____

_____

Interpersonal Effectiveness

Putting It All Together

Interpersonal effectiveness isn't about mastering every conversation or always knowing the perfect thing to say. It's about staying *rooted in your values* while navigating the unpredictable dance between your inner world and someone else's.

Healthy communication isn't the absence of conflict, it's the **presence of connection**, even when tension arises. It's learning how to stay steady enough to listen, curious enough to understand, and honest enough to express your truth without abandoning yourself or shaming the other person.

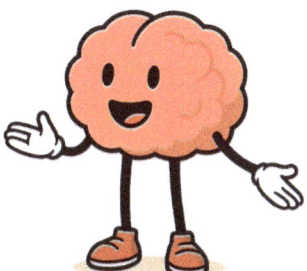

When you begin to integrate these skills; boundaries, communication, self-respect, emotional awareness, something subtle but profound happens: conversations start to feel less like battles and more like bridges. You stop trying to win and start trying to understand. You begin to notice that you can stay present even when things feel uncomfortable, because you're no longer trying to control the other person, you're choosing to regulate yourself.

Some days you'll get it wrong. You'll react before you think, or shut down when you wish you'd spoken up. *That's part of being human.*

What matters most is noticing the moment after, that quiet pause where awareness returns and you remind yourself that you can always try again.

Interpersonal effectiveness is a lifelong practice of returning to yourself.
It's the courage to be kind without losing your voice, to set boundaries without building walls, and to communicate with clarity even when your voice shakes.

The more you practice, the more you realise that these skills aren't just about other people, they're about you.

They're about choosing to meet the world with self-respect, curiosity, and compassion, one interaction at a time.

Shadow Work

Relationships reflect the stories we tell about love, safety, and worth. These prompts invite you to gently notice the patterns you replay when you feel unheard, unseen, or too much. Explore what it feels like to ask for what you need without apology, and to listen without losing yourself.

- When I express my needs, what emotions come up? Fear, guilt, frustration, shame?

_____
_____
_____
_____

- What situations make it hardest for me to say "no"? Why?

_____
_____
_____
_____

- When someone sets a boundary with me, how do I feel?

_____
_____
_____
_____

Shadow Work

- What kind of connection feels safest for me? Surface, deep, distant, constant? What does that say about my history with closeness?

_____
_____
_____
_____

- If I trusted that my needs were as important as others', what would I ask for today?

_____
_____
_____
_____

- Which of my boundaries are actually attempts to control others?

_____
_____
_____
_____

Integration
made easy

Moving Forward

Integration and Moving Forward

You've now explored the core DBT modules of mindfulness, distress tolerance, emotional regulation, and interpersonal effectiveness. Each one offers a piece of the puzzle, but their true power comes from how they work together.

Growth isn't about mastering a single skill; it's about weaving them into the rhythm of your daily life.

Think of these practices like a toolkit. Some days you'll need grounding and mindfulness. Other days, you'll lean on distress tolerance or boundary work. The goal isn't to use every tool at once, but to know which one to reach for when life starts to feel heavy. Over time, these skills begin to overlap, blending naturally into how you think, feel, and communicate.

Progress in emotional regulation isn't linear. There will be days when you feel deeply regulated and others when it feels like you're back at square one. That's not failure, it is simply something to bring awareness to. Revisiting earlier modules isn't a setback; it's a sign of growth and integration. Each return brings new awareness and refinement.

A *"life worth living,"* as Marsha Linehan calls it, isn't about perfection or constant peace. It's about creating a life that feels meaningful, one that aligns with your values and allows you to respond to life's challenges with compassion and clarity.

Take some time to reflect on what these practices have taught you about yourself. Which skills feel natural? Which still needs practice? How do you want to bring them into the next chapter of your life?

Reflection: Building Your Ongoing Practice

- What skill do I use most often, and why does it come naturally?
- Which skill do I avoid, and what might that avoidance be protecting me from?
- How has my understanding of myself and my emotions changed since starting this journey?
- What does a *"life worth living"* look like for me right now?

_____

_____

_____

_____

_____

Mindfulness

Wise Mind

When you listen to both heart and mind, you act from truth instead of reaction.

Emotion / **Wise** / **Logic**

Emotion Mind
Driven by feeling and impulse.
Fast, intense, protective.

Logic Mind
Focused on facts, patterns, and plans.
Clear, steady, structured.

Wise Mind
The calm space where both sides are heard.
A quiet sense of inner truth.

Accessing Wise Mind

Pause. Breathe.
Notice both logic and emotion without choosing sides.
Ask yourself: "What do I know to be true, deep down?"

Grounding

- 5 things you can see
- 4 things you can touch
- 3 things you can hear
- 2 things you can smell
- 1 thing you can taste

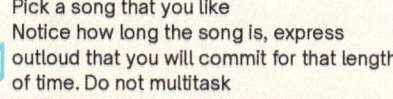

Pick a song that you like
Notice how long the song is, express outloud that you will commit for that length of time. Do not multitask
Softly sway to the rhythm, allow your body to move

Shift attention between different body parts
"Where is my nose?"
"Where are my feet?"

Do an awareness scan from head to toe
Notice where there is tension

Your brain is like a puppy, it is learning **recall**.
Like **gym** for your brain, you are **building muscle**.
Mindfulness does not mean "stillness" it means **presence**.
You can move and still be mindful

Curiosity

Approach life with curiosity not expectation

When you catch a critical thought, towards yourself or others, pause and notice the judgement
No need to fix or shame, simply notice it.
Then kindly ask yourself;
"Where did I learn this rule?"

The more grace we give others, the more understanding we have for ourselves

Judgement = Opinion + Moral criticism

to get out of **SHAME** → we need **UNDERSTANDING** → we get through **CURIOSITY**

Shift to Curiosity

Instead of deciding, start exploring.
Ask questions like:
- "What might this person's story be?"
- "Why does this bother me?"
- "What is my body trying to tell me right now?"

Acceptance

Radical Acceptance is the ability to completely accept your current reality as it is, without judgement.

- Notice resistance.
- Catch yourself in the "this shouldn't be happening" loop. That moment of awareness is the doorway in.
- Quietly state the facts: "This is what's happening right now."
- Acknowledge your emotions.
  Say to yourself, "I feel angry/sad/scared," without trying to change it.
- Relax the body.
  Loosen your jaw, open your hands, and breathe slowly.

**Choose acceptance again and again.
Radical acceptance is rarely a single moment**

Every time resistance returns, remind yourself;
"This is reality, and I can meet it."

Distress Tolerance

TIPP skill

For when emotions feel unbearable and you need to bring your thinking brain back online.

- **T** — **Temperature:** Cold on vagus nerve points, dunk head past temples, cold shower. Sudden temperature shifts help reconnect your thinking brain
- **I** — **Intense Exercise (Invigorate):** Move your body to release energy; run, shake, jump, dance, stretch. Match your breathing to your energy levels
- **P** — **Paced Breathing:** Inhale for 4, exhale for 6. Slower exhales activate calm. Match your energy levels to your breathing
- **P** — **Progressive Muscle Relaxation:** Tighten and release muscles from head to toe, reminding your body that it's safe.

TIPP helps reset your nervous system so you can respond, not react.

ACCEPTS Skill

Short-term distractions when emotions are overwhelming and problem-solving isn't possible yet.

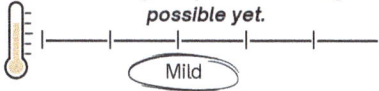

- **A** — **Activities:** engage your hands or body (draw, cook, walk).
- **C** — **Contribute:** help someone, send a message, volunteer.
- **C** — **Comparisons:** remind yourself of past challenges you've survived.
- **E** — **Emotions:** shift mood with humour, music, or uplifting videos.
- **P** — **Push Away:** take a break from what's distressing; revisit later.
- **T** — **Thoughts:** count, list, recite lyrics, focus on logic tasks.
- **S** — **Sensations:** ground yourself through strong sensory input (hold ice, smell citrus, eat something sour).

Distraction is not avoidance; it's giving your mind space to recover.

Self Soothe

Comfort the body through the five senses when you can't fix the situation.

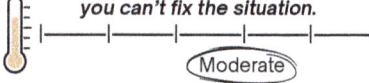

Have an easily accessible Self Soothing Sensory Box, both at home and something portable. Filled with things that bring you comfort

 Sight: Things you enjoy looking at; pictures, letters, art, colours

 Sound: Prepare a playlist that makes you feel good.

 Smell: Find smells that make you calm, candles, essential oils, a clothing item from a loved one.

 Taste: Have something grounding; mint, tea, or crunchy snacks.

 Touch: Wrap yourself in a blanket, hold a smooth stone, pet an animal, collect your favourite material.

Acceptance

Acceptance is a practice, not surrender. Each moment you choose it, you free yourself from unnecessary suffering.

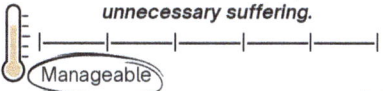

Relax your hands and turn your palms upward.
This small shift sends a calming signal through your body, helping your mind ease its grip on the moment.
You don't have to feel calm for the posture to work, letting your body soften creates space for everything else to follow.

 Soften your face and let the corners of your mouth lift slightly.
This gentle shift signals your nervous system to settle.
You don't have to feel calm for the posture to help, the body leads, the mind follows at its own pace.

Emotional Regulation

Understanding Emotions

Emotional regulation is about acknowledging our emotions and regulating our behaviours

- **Emotions are signals**, not problems to fix. They tell you something about your needs, values, or boundaries.
- **Every feeling has a function**: fear protects, sadness releases, anger defends, joy connects.
- **Name what you feel**; use your Feelings Wheel, describe sensations in your body through words, art, or music.

Describing your emotion gives your brain a sense of clarity and control.

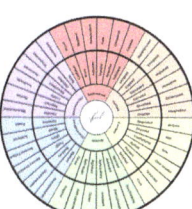

Pause for ten seconds and notice one physical sensation in your body.

Ask yourself;

"What might this be trying to tell me?"

Check The Facts

Separate what happened from what your emotions are telling you happened.

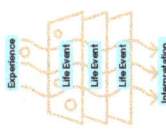

Our Life Filter influences how we interpret situations, sometimes we have to separate fact from past emotional experiences

Describe the situation simply sticking only to the known facts.
(Who, what, where, when)

- What do I know for sure?
- What assumptions am I adding?
- Is my emotional reaction based on the now or my past?

"Does this emotion fit the facts?"
If **yes** - act with it (cry, express, communicate).
If **no** - use **OPPOSITE ACTION** (approach instead of avoid, soften instead of fight).

Listen to your body, because our brains can lie, but our bodies don't know how.

Feeling Your Feelings

Rebuild trust and safety in your body, so that your emotions can move instead of getting stuck

- **Emotions live in the body**; not just in thoughts.
- **Notice** where the feeling shows up: your chest, stomach, throat, hands.
- **Stay with the sensation**, even for a few seconds longer than usual.
- **Breathe gently** into that space to show your brain it's safe to feel.

You don't have to understand it to allow it.

Take a double breath in through your nose, then exhale slowly through your mouth.
Say quietly: "I can feel this and still be safe."

Rebuilding trust and connection with our body takes time and effort.

Building Resilience

Assess why you might be having difficulty practicing Emotional Regulation;

- **Physical** health: is my body ok? Am I in pain?
- **Limit** triggers: Does my brain feel unsafe?
- **Eat** well: Have I had enough water and nutrients?
- **Avoid** substances: Am I under the influence?
- **Sleep**: Has my brain had time to recharge?
- **Exercise**: Has my body been able to move?

If you only ever remove negative coping methods without adding positive experiences your life will feel empty

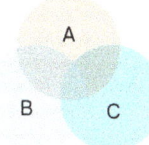

- **Accumulate** small, positive moments daily.
- **Build mastery** with small, consistent progress.
- **Cope ahead** by mentally rehearsing challenges.

"What small thing helped me feel more like myself today?"

Interpersonal Effectiveness

Identify
Identify your communication style

- People-Pleasing (Fawning): Prioritising others' needs over your own to avoid conflict.
- Avoidant (Withdrawing): Pulling away or shutting down instead of expressing emotions.
- Aggressive (Defensive/Controlling): Expressing needs forcefully or using guilt to get what you want.
- Passive-Aggressive: Indirectly expressing frustration rather than openly stating needs.

How can I be more assertive and balanced?

Identify your motivation

- What am I trying to get this person to understand?
- What would be the perfect outcome from this conversation?
- Am I willing to listen to their ideas?
- Am I willing to compromise?

We cannot change what we have not identified.

Assert
Boundaries are needed for healthy relationships

Boundaries vs Expectations vs Rules

Boundaries = *Self-directed*
→ About your own actions and limits
→ Protects your well-being
"If this happens, I will…"

Expectations = *Other-directed*
→ Hopes or wishes for how others behave
→ Requires communication, not control
"I hope you'll be honest with me."

Rules = *Control-based*
→ Attempts to manage someone else's behaviour → Often breeds resentment or fear
"You're not allowed to…"

Quick Check:
Am I setting this to honour myself, or to control someone else?

If it's to honour yourself, it's *a boundary*.

Communicate
Once we know what we need, we must ask

- Describe the situation (state the facts)
- Express how you feel about it
- Assert what you need clearly
- Reinforce why this benefits both sides
- Mindful (stay on topic)
- Anchor (be confident even if you don't feel it)
- Negotiate if needed (compromise)
  - Speak honestly.
  - Listen fully.
  - Look for solutions that protect connection and self-respect.
  - If things get tense, pause, regulate, and return when you feel grounded.

Communication / Compromise / Comprehension

Resolve
Protect relationships while communicating:.

- **G** **Gentle:** Speak with calm energy; regulate before you respond.
- **I** **Interested:** Be curious rather than defensive.
- **V** **Validate:** Acknowledge their feelings and your own.
- **E** **Engaged:** Stay open and steady even when the topic feels hard.

Keep your integrity during conflict.

- **F** **Fair:** Respect both your needs and theirs.
- **A** **Accountable:** Own your part without over-apologising.
- **S** **Steadfast:** Hold your boundaries and values.
- **T** **Truthful:** Speak from authenticity, not fear.

Integration

Shadow Work

Your shadow is made of the parts you once hid to stay safe: anger, desire, pride, creativity, softness, vulnerability, the need to be seen.

These parts never disappeared; they learned to speak in different ways. Shame, jealousy, irritation, or defensiveness are often signals that a hidden part wants attention.

Try asking:
- What am I afraid others will see in me?
- When did I learn that showing this part was unsafe?
- What would it mean to understand this part instead of shutting it down?

Get comfortable with asking why:
- Why do I think that?
- Why do they believe that?
- Is this belief still relevant now?

Shadow work grows through curiosity. Each question opens a little more room for honesty, understanding, and choice.

IFS

When a strong reaction surfaces, pause and ask:
- Who inside feels this way?
- What is this part trying to protect me from?
- How can I let it know I'm listening?

Managers
Keep things in control.

Firefighters:
Act fast to stop emotional pain.

Exiles
Carry the pain we had to hide

Self
The calm, compassionate core within you

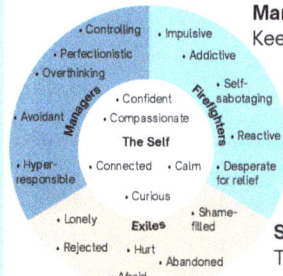

Try this:
Identify the part and say;
"Thank you for protecting me, but I can take it from here"

Relationship with self

The most important relationship you'll ever have is with yourself.
Start by giving yourself space to be human.

A gentle practice
Pause and breathe.
Acknowledge: "This is hard."
Remember that struggle happens to everyone.
Ask: "Do I need comfort or action?"

Build trust with yourself
- Keep small promises like drinking water.
- Say the action before you do it to rebuild "I say, I do."
- Get to know yourself
- Ask questions. Notice what you enjoy.
- Treat yourself with curiosity and patience.

A softer place to begin
You don't need self-love to start.
Begin with being slightly interested in who you are.

Making it work

Some days your skills will feel natural. Other days they'll feel far away. Both belong in the process.

Your tools:
Check the Facts when your mind starts filling in the blanks.
Radical Acceptance when life moves in its own direction.
Wise Mind when choices feel tangled.
Values when you need to remember what matters.
Mindfulness when you feel disconnected.
Shadow Work when patterns repeat and ask for attention.
IFS when your inner parts are pulling in different directions.
Distress Tolerance when you just need to get through the moment.
Boundaries when your peace starts depending on someone else's comfort.

I am learning. And that's enough.

www.ingramcontent.com/pod-product-compliance
Lightning Source LLC
Chambersburg PA
CBHW061729070526
44583CB00024B/3062